BOURBON ST.

ONE
WAY

GOD'S SUPER SALESMAN

"The Chaplain of Bourbon Street"
Bob Harrington

GOD'S SUPER SALESMAN

BROADMAN PRESS / NASHVILLE, TENNESSEE

© Copyright 1970 • Broadman Press
All rights reserved

Second Printing
ISBN: 0-8054-5529-9
4255-29

The opinions expressed in this book are those of
the author and are not necessarily in agreement with
nor in conflict with those of the publisher.

Library of Congress Catalog Card Number: 73–117310
Dewey Decimal Classification Number: 248.4
Printed in the United States of America

This book is gratefully dedicated to
My Lord and Savior Jesus Christ,
the greatest salesman mankind has known

and to
Liberty National Life Ins. Co., the first company
to offer me selling techniques.

And to four of the greatest salesmen in America.
Each played a most important part in my life
as a salesman for God
Fred Roan, Big Three Motors, Mobile, Alabama
Dr. J. D. Grey, First Baptist Church,
New Orleans, Louisiana
Bill Taylor, Taylor Machine Works,
Louisville, Mississippi
Rev. Jimmy Stroud, Memphis Union
Mission, Memphis, Tennessee

Contents

Preface

On February 8, 1961, I was ordained into the ministry as an "Evangelist." My pastor, Dr. J. D. Grey, presented me, as a gift from the First Baptist Church of New Orleans, Louisiana, a beautiful black morocco leather Scofield Reference Bible, and he wrote inside the Bible this Scripture:

> *But watch thou in all things,*
> *endure afflictions, do the work*
> *of an evangelist, make full proof*
> *of thy ministry.*
>
> 2 Timothy 4:5

Since that day, with the help of my Lord, my family, my dedicated staff, and many friends in Christ, I have tried to make full proof of my ministry. In this book I will attempt to share some of this proof. In reading these helpful hints you will soon realize that I'm not a theologian in any sense of the word, but just a simple sinner saved by the grace of God through my personal faith in Jesus Christ.

Bill Cannon, inspirational book editor with Broadman Press, said: "Bob Harrington, in this book let the reader get inside you, feel your emotions, your how's, your why's. This book could be a new thrust in evangelism. Open yourself up for others." This I have attempted to do. It is my prayer that, after reading this book, you will be more like Jesus would have you to be for Him—and less like you have been for yourself.

BOB HARRINGTON
(*Saved 4–15–58*)

GOD'S SUPER SALESMAN

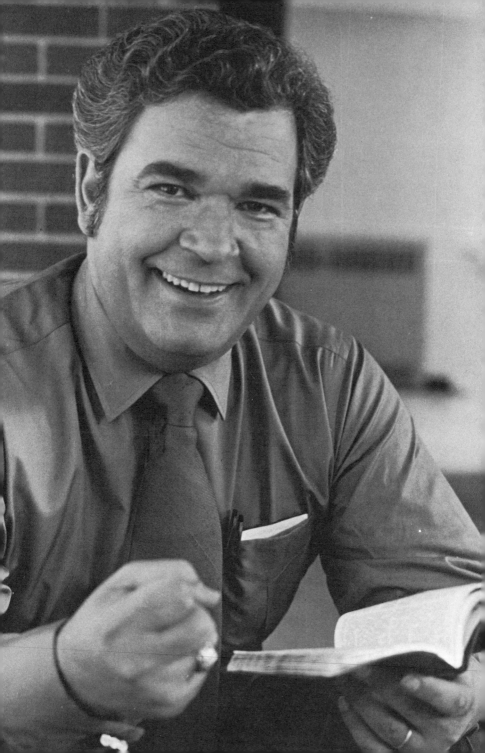

1. GO! Spell It Right!

If I had to use one word to describe my being called "God's Super Salesman," that word would have to be "GO!" From that night, April 15, 1958, 8:45 P.M., on the seventh pew, singing the fifth verse of "Just as I Am," in the Baptist Church of Sweet Water, Alabama, I have been going. Not just traveling (100,000–200,000 miles each year), but going with a purpose: to help carry out the command given to me and every born-again, blood-washed believer by my Lord and Saviour Jesus Christ in his Holy Word, "Go ye into all the world, and preach [sell] the gospel [my product] to every creature [my prospects]" (Mark 16:15).

Many wonderful things have taken place in my life since that new birth date in 1958, that is . . . after I started going. Immediately after my conversion I started going and telling what Jesus had done for me, and I haven't stopped yet—and don't plan to until the trumpet of the Lord shall sound, or until I move inside that Eastern Gate to begin my first 10,000 years with my Lord.

My first year was filled with "GO" and the leadership of the precious Holy Spirit. Each new plateau of growth or success was in direct result to my being obedient to his command of "Go."

Three days after my miraculous conversion I surrendered my life to preach the gospel, the good news that Jesus saves.

Six months after being saved I was invited by Evangelist Eddie Martin of Lancaster, Pennsylvania to go with him and

The night the mayor of New Orleans officially proclaimed Bob "The Chaplain of Bourbon Street." In Bob's first office.

help in his crusades. This man is one of God's choice servants. Does he go? To my knowledge during the six months Eddie let me work with him I don't remember one day he was not going from house to house witnessing and winning souls to Christ. Of all the evangelists I have met I don't know of anyone I would have enjoyed working with or learning from more than my dear friend, Eddie Martin. Thanks, Eddie!

One year after that life-changing night, I was in New Orleans serving in dual capacity: student at the New Orleans Baptist Theological Seminary and serving as assistant to the Pastor, of the First Baptist Church, Dr. J. D. Grey.

I didn't have someone come to my apartment and proclaim me "The Chaplain of Bourbon Street." This was the result of my going.

My first appearance on the Art Linkletter CBS-TV House Party came as a result of my going to Hollywood and letting Art's agent, Dick Pettit, know who I was and what I had to

offer his audience of sixteen million.

This great word "GO" keeps coming to me in each and every idea my Lord lets me develop. Look at "GO!" You can't spell "GOD" without "GO." You can't spell "GOOD" without "GO." You can't spell "GOSPEL" without "GO." When you know who you are, where you're going, and what you're doing, then "GO, MAN, GO" for Jesus. In Dayton, Ohio a young high school student introduced me as "a man on the go, go for God."

The command of Christ to GO has become an imperative instead of an elective by many of his followers. "You've got to *go*, to *know*, to *grow*" is the motto of my real friend in Christ, W. A. Taylor, Sr., of Taylor Machine Works in Louisville, Mississippi, who took his last GO in May, 1968 by going to heaven.

To keep from becoming a sterile, non-productive Christian (or salesman) don't ever let the "GO" go.

Go! Spell It Right! ···❖{15}❖···

Hanging on my office wall is an 8 x 10 black and white photograph of Henderson Belk, Charlotte, North Carolina, Executive Vice President of Belk Department Stores, with this inscription: "To my good saved friend, Bob Harrington, a man on the go who knows where he's going."

By the way, our Lord didn't promise us the road we would go on would be easy and smooth going. . . . Sure there are bumps on my road and yours, but I'd rather hit these bumps with Jesus serving as my Holy Shock Absorber than to be alone and possibly blow-out or end up in the ditch. (Just be sure to keep your steering mechanisms oiled with prayer and Holy Spirit strength!)

When Christ commanded us to be lights of the world, he had in mind brilliant beacons, not spiritual lightning bugs.

To defy Christ's command of GO is no worse than to ignore it. I have visited many churches with non-going leadership who say to me, "This is a hard city. We can't get sinners to come out to hear the gospel." I quickly reply, "This is a hard church. You can't get the Christians to go out after the sinners."

Jimmy Waters, pastor of Mabel White Memorial Baptist Church in Macon, Georgia, told his audience one night during

Bob takes the gospel to the need! Here he preaches in the "Sho-Bar" night club on Bourbon Street.

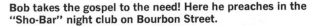

our four-day crusade when the crowd became so big we had to hold "double-headers," "If reincarnation were true, and Bob Harrington came back as a bird dog, I guarantee you he wouldn't be a setter."

One of the most challenging messages Eddie Martin ever preached to me was: "GO—Spell It Right." He said you don't spell "GO": G-I-V-E, P-R-A-Y, A-T-T-E-N-D, B-U-I-L-D, T-E-A-C-H, S-T-U-D-Y. He said all of these words and actions are good, but they do not replace God's command to us to "GO."

Joyce, my wife and prayer partner, said for me to tell you this: "You can't spell 'GONE' without 'GO' and you can't spell 'GOOD-BYE' without 'GO.'" She actually believes that I "GO" more from home and family than I come home.

Why do I start this book with an emphasis upon "GO?"

Because every following chapter develops—in one way or another—the things that are involved if a salesman for Christ really is to "GO" for God. This is the reason for chapters on alcohol, sex, sin, motivations, image. But hear me right. I am an evangelist, a "Super Salesman" for God, not a writer of neat little theories. I am accustomed to winning real people to Jesus Christ in real situations. This book reflects that. I am trying to take you inside me. I am trying to share with you the glory of selling for Christ, so I'm going to do it my way. I'm going to speak from my heart, I'm going to quote other people, I'm sharing with you pictures from our files. You will not find the following pages presenting a "definitive tome on evangelism." I will be hitting the high spots. I will be (apparently) jumping from one thing to another. But everything I say will be my way of developing the idea of "GO."

This is my personal testimony. Hear me right.

Remember, it's my prayer for you that you not only be a hearer and doer of the Word, but also a goer with the Good News. May God bless you as you "GO."

(PAGE 18) Brother Bob performs a wedding ceremony in "The Court of Two Sisters" in New Orleans, marrying a trumpet player to a dancer.

17

2. That Wonderful Sex Drive

The wonderful emotion of sex (sex drive) has back of it the possibility of three God-given potentials. They are:

1. The perpetuation of mankind.
2. The maintenance of health. (As a therapeutic agency, it has no equal.)
3. The change of mediocrity into genius through proper control.

Sex desire is the most powerful of human desires. When driven by this desire, men develop keeness of imagination, courage, willpower, persistence, and creative ability unknown to them at other times. So strong and impelling is the desire for sexual contact that men freely run the risk of life and reputation to indulge it.

The desire for sexual expression is inborn and natural. The desire cannot and should not be submerged or eliminated. When driven by this emotion, men become gifted with a super power for action. Destroy the sex glands, whether in man or beast, and you have removed the major source of action.

The desire for sex expression comes at the head of the list of stimuli which most effectively "step up" the mind and start the "wheels" of physical action.

The human mind responds to stimulation. Among the greatest and most powerful of these stimuli is the urge of sex. When properly guided, this wonderful driving force is capable of lifting men into that higher sphere of thought and accomplishments.

Name, if you can, a single man in all history of civilization who achieved outstanding success in any calling who was not driven by a well-developed sex nature. There never has been and never will be a great leader, preacher, or salesman lacking in this driving force of sex.

Surely no one will misunderstand these statements to mean that all who are highly sexed become successes. Far from becoming successes because of great sex desires, the majority of men become failures through misunderstanding and misuse of this great driving force, some falling to the status of the lower animals.

The most powerful of all human emotions is that of sex. Any emotion is a powerful motivator. People are influenced in their actions, not by facts so much as by "feelings." But the most powerful motivator is sex. The public speaker, orator, preacher, lawyer, or salesman who is lacking in sex energy is a "flop" as far as being able to influence others is concerned.

The Christian who knows how to let the Holy Spirit lead in his sex thoughts and directs this power with as much enthusiasm and determination as he would apply to its physical purpose is well on his way toward success.

Control of our wonderful sex drive needs more than just willpower. We need the direction of God through His Holy Spirit to lead, guide, and direct us.

The emotion of sex is a virtue only when used intelligently and with discrimination, or, in better words, "used for the glory of God." It may be misused, and often is, by the "lost and saved," to such an extent that it debases instead of enriches both body and mind.

The road to success, once you find the will of God for your life and get into it, consists of development, control, and use of

Mr. and Mrs. Harrington
with daughters
Rhonda (LEFT) and Mitzi.

sex, love, and romance. Even Dean Martin knows, "You're Nobody Till Somebody Loves You."

Man's greatest motivating force is his desire to please woman! Do you believe this? Ask yourself, and analyze your answer. Men may be "giants" with indomitable willpower when dealing with other men but they are easily managed by the woman of their choice.

Most salesmen I know are super-sexative. Clerks are usually cold conformists. The apostle Peter, the apostle Jesus loved so much, was a super-sexed man. He was warming with a maiden by an open fire while the soldiers were taking Jesus to Pilate. King David and Samson must have been two great salesmen. Samson found his uncontrolled sex to be grinding, binding, and blinding. What a great life he could have lived and given had he controlled his sex drive. Of the three categories of sin our Bible describes, the lust of the flesh has gotten to more salesmen than any other sin.

Keep your hands off that pretty secretary!

Could it have been Daniel was not really in a den with lions but at an office party with the girls?

When it comes to the sex question, I've said many times, "My Lord saved me but he didn't ruin me." My sex drive has been much stronger since I've been saved (April 15, 1958), but thank God the Holy Spirit has helped me as he did Paul to control and properly to direct this wonderful drive. "There hath no temptation taken you but such as is common to man: but God is faithful, who will not suffer [permit] you to be

Bob Harrington speaks to the Cleveland Browns football team.

tempted above that ye are able; but will with the temptation also make a way to escape, that ye may be able to bear it" (1 Cor. 10:13).

3. A Sure Cure for Alcoholism

As a God-called evangelist I'm invited to some of the greatest churches in the world. One of these is Thomas Road Baptist Church, Lynchburg, Virginia, where Jerry Falwell is the founder and pastor. In thirteen years this church grew from a handful to 3500 attending Sunday School and church. Jerry Falwell is one of God's best salesmen. Because of its importance, and because Jerry states the case so well, may I share with you one of his messages?

"A Sure for Alcoholism"

TEXT: Proverbs 23:29–35—"Who hath woe? who hath sorrow? who hath contentions? who hath babbling? who hath wounds without cause? who hath redness of eyes? They that tarry long at the wine; they that go to seek mixed wine. Look not thou upon the wine when it is red, when it giveth his colour in the cup, when it moveth itself aright. At the last, it biteth like a serpent, and stingeth like an adder. Thine eyes shall behold strange women, and thine heart shall utter perverse things. Yea, thou shalt be as he that lieth down in the midst of the sea or he that lieth upon the top of a mast. They have striken me, shalt thou say, and I was not sick; they have beaten me, and I felt it not: when shall I awake? I will seek it yet again."

Almost every family in America is affected either directly or indirectly by the curse of alcoholism. Very few families have not tasted the bitterness of a home in which a drinker lives. Conservative estimates tell us that between five and seven million Americans confess to be alcoholics today. More and more our nation is facing a real crisis with alcoholism. Our young people are being taught to drink even before high school days. Mothers and daddies drink right before their children. Many of our national leaders and professional people are now drinkers. Drinking is no longer the curse of poor people. The rich and poor alike are falling into the snares of liquor. We are now being told that alcoholism is a disease. We are being led to believe that certain people drink because they are sick and cannot help it. In this message I will deal with the biblical viewpoint toward drinking. I will try to answer the questions that people are asking about alcoholism.

Is Alcoholism a Disease?

In the first place, the word "alcoholism" is not found in the Bible. This word has been invented in the last few years to dilute the awfulness of the sin of drunkenness. We have, for more than six years, operated the Elim Home for Alcoholics. Mr. and Mrs. Ray Horsley are

Crowds love Bob.

Bob never misses
an opportunity to witness
when visiting night clubs
looking for prospects for Jesus.

presently directing this work which is located in the Lynchburg area. At this home we offer no medical help. Men who come to Elim must come voluntarily, seeking spiritual help only. If alcoholism is a disease, why has there been found no medical way of treating it? There is no doctor, no medicine, no hospital, and no medical treatment which has ever uncovered the answer to alcoholism. Millions of dollars are being spent annually by men and women seeking deliverance through medical help in hospitals, etc.

Alcoholism in the Bible is actually called "drunkenness." In Romans 13:13 and Galations 5:21, the Bible lashes out against the wickedness of drunkenness. The idea that alcoholism is a disease simply affords a crutch for those who wish to drink without guilt. It is true that a man or woman can drink so excessively that his or her body begins to crave and depend upon alcoholic beverages for life itself. The same thing can be said about drug addiction. There are those who are completely addicted to gambling. However, this does not constitute a disease. Alcoholism is neither hereditary nor contagious. Don't ever blame anyone else for your drinking. If you drink, it is because you have chosen to do so. You cannot shove the blame to any of your friends or relatives who offered you something to drink.

Is Social Drinking a Sin?

I hear people who constantly say: "I can handle my drinks." In this age of drunkenness it is most unpopular to take a stand against liquor, wine, and beer. A Christian, however, must stand where the Bible stands. It doesn't matter what my opinion or your opinion about the matter is. The important thing is—"What does the Bible say?" In our text for this message you have already read Proverbs 23:29–35. In these verses of our text God forbids our drinking any form of fermented or alcoholic beverage. We are even forbidden to look upon it—verse 31. These verses and many others in the Bible strictly forbid a Christian partaking of alcoholic beverages to any degree. When God speaks, the matter is *settled!* Sin is transgression of God's law. Therefore if a Christian drinks alcoholic beverages to any degree, he has transgressed God's law and is therefore guilty of sin. No pastor, deacon, church officer, choir member, or Christian worker has any right performing his Christian duty if he is guilty of drinking. A teacher or worker in Thomas Road Church would be dismissed immediately for committing such a sin. The Bible says they would be "blind leaders of the blind." No drunkard ever set out in life to become a drunkard. Every drunkard took his first drink. Perhaps it was just a social drink offered him by a friend. How we need to teach our young people today the perils and the sin of drinking!

Is There Any Hope?

We have already stated that there is no medical deliverance for alcoholism. We have said that alcoholism is pure sin against God. It is true that drunkards mistreat their families and friends. It is true that people who live around drinkers live a most miserable life. But the chief sin of drinking is the sin against god. There has never been but one cure for sin. In 1 John 1:7 we read: "The blood of Jesus Christ his Son cleanseth us from all sin." The hope of the drunkard is the same as the hope of all sinners. Jesus Christ and his shed blood present the only answer.

Drinking is in reality no worse than any other sin. All sin grieves God whether it be lying, dishonesty, immorality, or any sin of the flesh—it is all transgression of God's law. It only happens that drinking presents a more outward manifestation for the world to gaze upon. The same remedy that works for all sinners also works for drunkards.

I have known hundreds of men and women whom the Lord has delivered from the curse of drunkenness. I know what the gospel can do. However no drunkard can be delivered against his own will. If you are reading this message today and happen to be in the grips of liquor, you must first see and acknowledge your sinful condition. Before God can find you, you must admit that you are lost. Your worst sin is not drinking, but *rebellion against God!* You drink because you are a sinner by nature. God loves you and desires to give you a new nature. This new nature is Christ himself. He will actually come to live within you, giving you the power necessary to live the victorious Christian life. You will not have to stop drinking by willpower; God's power will deliver. As a poor, lost, hopeless sinner, a drunkard must fall before the Lord seeking salvation and mercy. God will never turn you away.

After you have trusted the Lord Jesus Christ as your Saviour and God, it is necessary then to feed your spiritual life. We are told repeatedly to study God's Word. This is food for the soul. We also need regular fellowship with Christian people. The church plays a great role here. Every child of God needs to spend much time in prayer daily. Even after God has saved the drunkard, the new Christian still has a human body and is capable of sin. Jesus Christ, who lives in the born-again drunkard, desires to rule from within the human spirit the entire life. We are more than conquerors through Him who loved us. Sin does not have dominion over us now. We must live constantly in dependence upon the blessed Holy Spirit who abides in our bosom. As we look to Him, studying the Word, spending much time in prayer, attending every service at God's House, we may expect the Lord to keep us daily from the temptation of the Evil One. God can do for you what He has done for thousands of others.

Trust Him today. If you do place your faith and trust in the Lord Jesus Christ as the result of reading this message, we would like to hear from you in order to offer additional help. Write me: Jerry Falwell, Box 1111, Lynchburg, Virginia.

I have used Jerry's message (with his permission, of course) not because I do not have something to say about alcoholism, but because Jerry says it so well. Remember, I am trying to tell you how to be a super salesman for Christ. Just as you cannot be one unless you have learned to handle the sex drive, you cannot be one unless you are right on the alcohol question.

But neither can you be a super salesman unless you have "Holy Boldness."

We'll look at that next.

Bob never misses an opportunity to preach the gospel.

4. Holy Boldness

I don't believe there is a human being alive today that I would be afraid to witness to for my Christ. Paul told Timothy in 2 Timothy 1:7, "For God hath not given us the spirit of fear; but of power, and of love, and of a sound mind." I recommend this attitude to you. I think there are three things in your life that keeps you from having "Holy Boldness." First, wilful sin in your life. Second, neglect of Bible study, prayer, faithfulness to Christ and his church. Third, timid worry over what "others" may think or say.

I believe I have preached under practically every existing situation I am conscious of . . . churches, schools, civic clubs, garden clubs, social clubs, Mardi Gras crowds, mob riots, motorcycle gangs, orgies, night clubs, honky-tonks, television, radio, battlegrounds in Viet Nam, Knights of Columbus, B'nai Brith, Ku Klux Klans, leftist, rightist, militants, high school pep rallies, college seminars, on stage with exotic dancers, following six topless girl dancers in Atlanta's Domino Lounge, horse shows, drag strips, wrestling matches, boxing—and on and on. Sometimes I had mixed emotions, and many times I was excited, but not one time did my Lord fail me. Always he blessed my witness.

John the Baptist is a good example of "Holy Boldness." He went to see the king, without invitation or warning, and pointed his finger at the adultery involved. The liberals say, "Yes, but this cost him his head." Yes, but he made the Book. Jesus said this of John, "None greater ever came from woman."

Paul and Silas had "Holy Boldness" on the streets (not just in the buildings behind stained windows) of Philippi and continued in this bold spirit in the jail past midnight. I know these men must not have been too church-centered in their faith, or at midnight, instead of shouting, they would have been pouting because their pastor hadn't paid them a visit. This boldness paid off, as it always does, in the jailer and his entire family getting saved (and probably many of those in the jail). Our sin-sick society today will not respond to a timid, half-hearted, false humility type of witness. We must come on strong with much dedicated Holy Spirit-led witnessing and soul-winning for our Lord Jesus who will truly bless our "Holy Boldness" when it is for his glory.

"Holy Boldness" does not come easy. You must develop muscles in your soul by exercise of your faith or simply telling others of your personal salvation experience with Christ. In 1958, after my conversion, my Lord led me to men like Fred Roan and Luke McDaniels, two saved used-car salesmen in Mobile who helped me to launch out into the deep. At this time

Bob preaches in the county prison in Macon, Georgia.

The night Bob preached to 1,500 people in this tent a storm in the community blew the roof off the airport building down the road—but the tent was unharmed.

I had never prayed in public. I had never heard of a soul-winner, much less met one. Those first few months as my spiritual muscles were developing proved to be tremendous.

There is much that can be said, preached, and written about "Holy Boldness," but the only way you will ever have it is to start by witnessing for Jesus. You will never develop this type of boldness until you completely turn loose and let Jesus work through you. Right now, stop, and tell someone near that Jesus loves him.

Regards
Frank P Sanford

Frank Sanford, Liberty National Life Insurance, was Bob's boss for two years.

5. Clerk or Salesman

A *salesman* is a man whose work is selling.

A *clerk* is a person whose work is waiting on customers and selling goods in a store.

Too many Christians are "Clerks for Christ" just waiting at home, school, job, or church for someone to *come and ask* about Christ. Christians should be out in the world telling and selling the wonderful story of love. Jesus said, "Go and tell . . ." When *we* go, *they* come to Him. Many of the clerks for Christ today are referred to as "Liberals." I had much rather die today being a salesman for my Lord than to be alive tomorrow as an order-taking liberal.

I believe once a man (young or old) receives a divine call from God to preach the gospel of Jesus Christ, he should start developing his salesmanship. Get a part-time job in selling as you study. Many of the preacher students at New Orleans Baptist Theological Seminary work as salesmen for Sears while attending school. This is good! I think a selling job is more profitable in the long run for our Lord and ourselves than having a weekend church (unless the preacher student has had selling experience prior to his calling—as I did.

I believe Bible schools and seminaries should require courses in salesmanship and sales management for all students. The schools offer speech, but adding salesmanship courses would help speaking.

Paul the apostle was a great salesman, surpassed only by

Jesus Christ. Everyone Paul met was a prospect. He went everywhere with his product (the gospel) selling salvation to sinners.

The apostles we remember most are the ones who were salesmen. The others are just mentioned in the Bible and rarely remembered. Now I know there will always be more clerks than salesmen, but why? I believe the weakest Christian could be a salesman if he would let Christ help him (Phil. 4:13).

I have often been told, "You can't sell something unless you're sold on it yourself." With this in mind I should be a great salesman of Christianity, because I'm sure sold on Christ!

I don't want to be sidetracked by others. Whatever or whoever has my attention has me. I have given all of my attention to Christ and thank God, he has me!

If there's any man in God's kingdom the devil wants sidetracked it's the man on the go for God, the salesman. Many times the devil will try to make exciting offers to get you, the salesman, off the field into the home office, denominational positions, and so forth. I must admit I've had some attractive, lucrative offers from many sources, but so far, with the precious leadership of the Holy Spirit, I've stuck to my selling. By the way, so did the apostle Peter and Paul the apostle, two top salesmen.

In my ministry I have as my Executive Director, Steve Callahan, who has a masters degree from Harvard University in Sales Management. His job is to market and merchandise me, my LP records, books, radio and television programs, citywide crusades, and so forth. My Music Coordinator is Jack Price, who has had much selling experience. He must each week sell hundreds of new people on himself, my ministry, and our Christ. Oh, I pay these men well, and they will continue to get good raises as our Lord continues to bless.

Remember, I believe in success. I believe that the Lord intends for you to succeed. I believe he blesses you when you are successful. I have been told that I represent a new thrust in mass evangelism because of my emphasis upon success, that I am "highly success-oriented." Well, I don't know how "new" such an emphasis is. It seems to me that God has always wanted us to succeed and that we owe it to him to succeed.

I grant that, when I turned my life over to the Lord, I turned over to him the life of a salesman—a good salesman. (And I certainly do not intend to be less of a salesman for Jesus than I was for the secular world!) I see things the way a good salesman sees them, and no good salesman ever lived who was happy unless he closed the deal—made a success. But I contend that this is just exactly the attitude God expects of us, that he expects us to be salesmen, super salesmen, not clerks.

Don't be satisfied as a clerk—follow Jesus closer and become a salesman and get those extra commissions (rewards and blessings)!

6. Now That You Are Saved . . . What's Next?

I personally believe it is most important when we lead someone to Christ, or when someone responds to a local church invitation to accept Christ, that we do all we can to help this person grow in the grace and knowledge of Jesus Christ. May I share with you the content of a tract I try to place into the hand of each person making a decision in our crusades. Much credit should be given to Rev. Harold Rawlings of Landmark Baptist Temple in Cincinnati, Ohio, for the shaping up of this tract.

Now That You Are Saved . . . What Next?

Your decision to receive Jesus as Saviour is the most important you will ever make. There is no greater joy in all the world than to know Christ personally, to know your sins are forgiven, and to have peace in your soul. You have been born again—born of the Spirit. A miracle has taken place in your life. You are a new creature: "Therefore if any man be in Christ, he is a new creature: old things are passed away; behold, all things are become new" (2 Cor. 5:17). God, the Creator of the universe, has become your Father. Now for the first time you are considered a child of God and Heaven is your eternal home.

Although your decision to become a Christian, is great and important, it is not all. It is but the beginning of a new life in Christ. When you were saved you were not immediately a full grown Christian, but a "babe in Christ." As a baby you are commanded to "grow" (2 Pet. 3:18). Everybody loves babies, but nobody wants them to stay in the nursery. Only by growing spiritually can you please God and glorify Him in your life.

In order to grow to maturity as a Christian you must be loyal and obedient to the commands of Christ. He said, "If ye love me, keep my commandments" (John 14:15). Some of these requirements are listed here in order that you may know what our Lord expects of His disciples.

(1). Be Baptized

Baptism is the first step of obedience for a new Christian. The first public act in the ministry of Jesus was His baptism by John the Baptist, in the river Jordan (Mat. 3:13–17). The New Testament teaches that baptism is an outward sign of an inward change (Rom. 6:4). It is a public confession and testimony of what has already taken place in your heart. Baptism is a burial and a resurrection. We are buried with Christ (immersed in water) in the likeness of his death, and we are raised with Christ in the likeness of his resurrection (Rom. 6:2–3). Not only does baptism picture the death, burial and resurrection of Christ, it also pictures the burial of the old sinful life and the resurrection of a new life in Christ. As a believer you should be baptized, not in order to be saved but because you are saved (Acts 8:35–40). It is a witness to your faith in Christ.

(2). Read Your Bible Daily

Jesus said, "Man shall not live by bread alone, but by every word that proceedeth out of the mouth of God" (Matt. 4:4). Just as you need physical food in order to sustain physical life, so you need spiritual food (the

Bible) to maintain spiritual life. We suggest you begin in the New Testament by reading the Gospel of John or Mark. Follow this with the book of Acts. Next, read Paul's Epistle to the Romans. The entire New Testament can be read in three months by reading three chapters a day. By reading three chapters of the Old Testament and one chapter of the New Testament each day, the whole Bible can be read in a year. Set aside a few moments early in each day for Bible study. Look for promises to claim and commands to obey, examples to follow and sins to avoid. Memorize key verses such as John 3:16. Your growth as a Christian will be directly related to your personal application of the Word of God.

(3). Pray Every Day

Jesus said, "Men ought always to pray" (Luke 18:1). In another place we read, "Pray without ceasing" (1 Thess. 5:17). You should form the habit of praying daily for definite people and specific things. A prayer list may

Standing room only! The crowd at the service held at the "Sho-Bar" nightclub during the SBC Convention in New Orleans.

Now That You Are Saved . . . What's Next? ⟶⟨43⟩⟵

Two advisers to Bob's ministry: (LEFT) Bill Taylor; (SEATED) W. A. Taylor, Sr.

prove helpful in making your prayers more meaningful. There is nothing too great and nothing too small to take to the Lord in prayer. Thank God for all he has done for you. Ask him for the strength and help you need to live for Jesus Christ.

(4). Witness for Christ

The greatest work in the world is soul winning and every Christian can and should bring others to the Saviour. Jesus said, "Ye shall be witnesses unto ME" (Acts 1:8). Try to speak naturally and cheerfully every day to someone about Christ. The Bible says, "He that winneth souls is wise." (Prov. 11:30). Remember that you witness by what you do as well as by what you say. At home, at work, at school, there should be something about you that's different—love, patience, understanding. Then tell someone about HIM who makes the difference.

(5). Tithe Your Income

Tithing (giving a tenth) of your income is the biblical method of supporting God's work. The Bible tells us,

Brother Bob in An Khe, Viet Nam with Chaplain Billy Lloyd. Over 100 men of the First Cavalry Division accepted Christ as Savior.

"Upon the first day [Sunday] of the week let every one of you lay by him in store, as God hath prospered him" (1 Cor. 16:2). God says to bring the tithe into the "storehouse," meaning the local church. Your church is your storehouse of spiritual food, blessing and service, so this is the proper place to give your tithe. "Bring ye all the tithes into the storehouse . . . and prove me now herewith, saith the Lord of hosts, if I will not open you the windows of heaven, and pour you out a blessing, that there shall not be room enough to receive it" (Mal. 3:10). The right use of money is a test of character. If you are dishonest toward God in money matters you cannot grow spiritually.

(6). Attend Church Regularly

The Christian life is not just our own private affair. It is to be a family affair, in which we enjoy fellowship with our Heavenly Father and with each other. Every Christian should unite with a local, Bible believing church and share its worship, its fellowship and its witness. If

Jesus loved the church enough to die for it (Eph. 5:25), this is sufficient reason for us to love and support it. Regular church attendance should be as much of a habit as eating. "Not forsaking the assembling of ourselves together" (Heb. 10:25) is a clear command of the Word of God. At the church services you will hear God's Word read, explained and applied to your every-day problems of life. God has ordained (set aside) men to minister and preach his Word. Every Christian, young and old, needs the inspiration and information gained in a church worship service. If you try to live the Christian life alone, failure will result. In unity there is strength. Through the church you can render service to a lost and dying world.

There is far more to the Christian life than what is included here, but, if these initial steps are carefully followed, you will find yourself growing more and more in the knowledge of our Lord and Saviour Jesus Christ.

Our crusades take our team to many places. Our primary concern is winning souls for Jesus Christ, but we do not believe the matter can be ended there. I may differ from some of my brethren in my emphasis upon "Super Salesmanship for Christ," but, having once won a man to Jesus, none of us can substitute any "new" way for the old pattern of spiritual growth. This should be as self-evident as the need to win souls. But self-evident truths are not always recognized. For instance, it should be self-evident that Christians ought to know how to win souls to Jesus. Yet you would be surprised at how many Christians do not know how to win souls.

So, let's see what we can do about that.

**Brother Bob with Art Linkletter on Art Linkletter's House Party,
CBS-TV, June 27, 1966.**

7. May I Help You to Win a Soul to Jesus?

Many people ask me, "Bob, how can I win someone to Christ?" In answer to this much-asked question, I wrote a tract. Here it is!

May I Help You to Win a Soul to Jesus?
Let's look at the soul winning approach of Jesus:

1. He believed that all men are worth saving.
2. He won their confidences.
3. He stimulated their interests (curiosities).
4. He deepened their curiosities into spiritual thirsts.
5. He confronted them boldly and inescapably with the question of sin.
6. He led them to turn from sin to faith in him.
7. He encouraged them to share their salvation experiences immediately with someone else.

Successful soul-winning demands that we sacrifice and agonize over lost souls. Genuine love and concern must undergird each presentation of the gospel. Knowing the mechanics of soul-winning is not enough. Soul-winners must be concerned with lost individuals not merely as statistics or potential church members, but as persons who are trying to find themselves, to find whom they are and where they are going.

Dwight L. Moody took soul-winning so seriously that he would not sleep at night until he had shared the saving power of Jesus Christ with at least one other person. Amy Carmichael, another dedicated soul winner, prayed:

"Oh for a passion of souls
Oh for a pity that yearns
Oh for a love that loves unto death
Oh for a heart that burns."

For too long our churches have retreated into the security of their four walls. They need to break through their niceties and encounter people with the gospel where they are and as they are. You can lead the way in your church. Don't wait for someone else to lead out; you shoe leather the gospel onto docks and into apartment houses, beauty shops, discount stores, and laboratories. Others will follow your example.

Becoming a disciple (learner, student) of Jesus is necessary, but never to mature past being a disciple is stagnation (spiritual dwarfism). Jesus makes disciples in order to send forth apostles (enlisting agents). Acts 1:8 says: "But ye shall receive power (disciple stage), after that the Holy Ghost is come upon you (fueling stage): and ye shall be witnesses (apostles) unto me both in Jerusalem (first with immediate family and other relatives), and in all Judea and in Samaria (friends, casual acquaintances, and strangers), and unto the uttermost part of the earth (foreign missions)."

Andrew discovered Jesus; he felt compelled (inwardly driven) to share Him with his brother. . . . John 1:42 says "He [Andrew] brought him [Peter] to Jesus." Winning souls to Jesus is urgently important. Leading men to Jesus is more pressing than securing doctors for cancerous patients or rushing firemen to hospital blazes. Men's eternal destinies are at stake.

**Bob is always witnessing.
And Bourbon Street
is a good place
to do it.**

May I Help You to Win a Soul to Jesus? ---◦◦{51}◦◦---

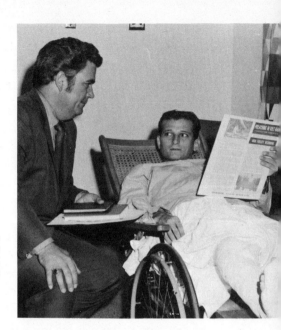

Bob talks to Charles L. West, Viet Nam returnee. (Photo by Sp5 Herrmann Pictorla Branvh, Ft. Benning, Ga.)

Bringing men into "oneness" with himself (reconciliation) meant more to Jesus than the splendors he had been sharing with the Father since before time began. The Bible indicates that the Son emptied himself of it all (glory). Willingly he resigned heavenly Sonhood to become Son of Man. He removed himself from ivory places to become part of our world of woe.

Before going further, are you in right relationship to Jesus Christ? Ask him into your life if you have never done so. Rededicate yourself to him if Satan has led you astray. Claim God's Spirit. Ask him to fill you, lead you, and use you to win a soul to Jesus Christ.

Let me share with you five verses which helped me win my first soul to Jesus:

Romans 3:23 "For all have sinned, and come short of the glory of God." (All men are sinners.)

Romans 6:23 "For the wages of sin is death; but the gift of God is eternal life through Jesus Christ our Lord." (The result of sin is death. Eternal life is a God-given gift.)

Romans 10:9–10 "That if thou shalt confess with thy mouth the Lord Jesus, and shalt believe in thine heart that God hath raised him from the dead, thou shalt be saved. For with the heart man believeth unto righteousness; and with the mouth confession is made unto salvation." (Confess your sin and believe with your heart.)

Romans 10:13 "For whosoever shall call upon the name of the Lord shall be saved." (Call on the Lord for salvation.)

8. Not Skin, But Sin

During a city-wide crusade in Hagerstown, Maryland, sponsored by Rev. Jimmy Resh's Rescue Mission, one of the crusade team members was Sam Dalton, a black-saved-layman who loves Jesus. His answer to our black-white race problem was printed for distribution and I now share it with you.

Not Skin But Sin

We live in a time of demonstrations which change not the heart or morals, but make headline news the world over. Yet the imperative demonstration is of the Holy Spirit and his power (1 Cor. 2:4). The best news may never reach headlines. Such is concerning the Lord Jesus Christ who came "to seek and to save that which was lost" (Luke 19:10); and "put away sin by the sacrifice of himself" (Heb. 9:26).

'Tis he alone who can change the ugly picture and plight of our times, for "if any man be in Christ, he is a new creature: old things are passed away; behold all things are become new" (2 Cor. 5:17).

In spite of good intentions, millions spent, the frantic efforts of legislators and law enforcers, the worst is yet to come; for every kingdom divided against itself shall be brought to desolation (Matt. 12:25); and "they that take the sword shall perish with the sword" (26:52).

So much talk as to Black, Green, White, and Student power, but the only message that shall change hearts is the gospel of Christ which "is the power of God unto salvation to every one that believeth" (Rom. 1:16).

Sad that a country so great, founded upon Christian principles, has deteriorated so because of a lack of faith in him who "upholding all things by the word of his power, when he had by himself purged our sins, sat down on the right hand of the Majesty on high" (Heb. 1:3). "Hatred stirreth up strifes: but love covereth all sins" (Prov. 10:12). Love that beareth, believeth, hopeth, endureth all things and never faileth, when practiced will solve the perplexing problems of our day (1 Cor. 13: 7–8). "He that loveth not knoweth not God; for God is love" (1 John 4:8).

While many make the issue "SKIN," the truth is the real issue is "SIN," and this is the cause of broken hearts, homes, and our nation being in the throes of chaos. Tradition binds while truth frees. The only answer, though despised in our times in general, is the love of God as manifested in Christ Jesus, who laid down his life for us; who "once suffered for sins, the just for the unjust, that he might bring us to God" (1 Pet. 3:18).

"Ye shall know the truth and the truth shall make you free" (John 8:32). 'Tis not a matter of class, but Christ. Not race but grace, and such is God's riches at Christ's expense (Eph. 2:8).

This peace is ours by simply putting our trust in the Lord Jesus Christ who knew no sin but was made to be sin for us "that we might be made the righteousness of God in him" (2 Cor. 5:21).

Thus as a Negro seeking not sympathy, or sensationalism, but indeed concerned about my fellow citizens regardless of nationality, and who knows without doubt, "for I know whom I have believed" (2 Tim. 1:12), that the Lord Jesus Christ who was delivered for our offences, and raised again for our justification, is the only answer for whatever the dilemma. I am convinced that trusting in him will do what men, methods, and means have thus far failed to do—and shall continue to fail in achieving as faith "is the victory that overcometh the world" (1 John 5:4). O that men would repent and be reconciled to God who is no respecter of persons!

Bob visiting a club in Wichita, Kansas and witnessing for Jesus

Friend of mine, the Lord Jesus says, . . . "He that heareth my word, and believeth on him that sent me, HATH everlasting life, and shall not come into condemnation; but is passed from death unto life" (John 5:24). "That if thou shalt confess with thy mouth the Lord Jesus, and shalt believe in thine heart that God hath raised Him from the dead, thou shalt be saved" (Rom. 10:9).

Do It Now!

For the Bible says, "Today, if ye will hear his voice, harden not your hearts" (Heb. 3:7–8). "Whosoever shall call upon the name of the Lord shall be saved" (Rom. 10:13).

(REPRINTED BY PERMISSION)

The young people
listen to Bob's
witness

Not Skin, But Sin ---❖{59}❖---

9. Is There Room for Non-Conformists?

Our crusades are non-sectarian. A Super Salesman for Christ wins souls to Jesus, not to a single denomination. Personally, of course, I am a loyal member of the Southern Baptist Convention. I have been asked many times how a "non-conformist" such as I am can fit into my own denomination. Rather than answer this in my own words, let me share with you a story from the Louisiana *Baptist Message,* April 2, 1964, two years after I was proclaimed "The Chaplain of Bourbon Street." (Reprinted by permission.)

By Wes Jackson

Do Baptists have room for non-conformists?

"Yes," says one of the most controversial Baptist preachers in all of Louisiana, Bob Harrington, who has gained fame in some quarters and notoriety in others as the "Chaplain of Bourbon Street" by setting up shop and preaching along that part of New Orleans' French Quarter once described by Billy Graham as "the middle of Hell."

Harrington, or "Big Daddy," as he is known, is a non-conformist when compared to most preachers, whom he says "look like accidents dressed up waiting for a place to happen."

Operating out of what used to be a Bourbon Street

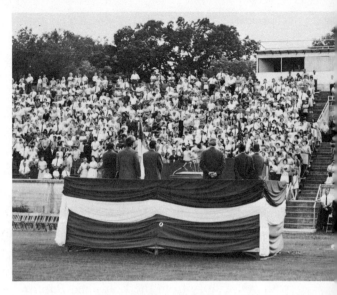

The multitudes
are still waiting
for the gospel

package liquor store, Harrington's activities consist of such unique situations as preaching the Gospel to an audience of strippers, barkers (doormen-hawkers), and night club owners from the stage of a strip-tease joint; preaching to winos and punch-drunk ex-pugilists at a combination gymnasium and bar, and performing services and weddings in a Vieux Carre patio-restaurant, the Court of Two Sisters.

Much of the criticism directed at Harrington has been two-fold: first for his surroundings as a minister, and, secondly, for his unorthodox and highly successful publicity which results from his unique methods.

As for his surroundings, Harrington, a husky, wavy-haired man who calls things as he sees them, has stated that God wants us all to be Fishers of Men. Where else, he asks, can there be found a bigger fishhole than on Bourbon Street?

When questioned directly about his location and the people whom he is trying to reach, Harrington says,

"Jesus saved only sinners; not once do we read of Him saving a person who was already a Christian. Why, look at the people who followed Christ at the beginning— Was Saul on his way back from a Brotherhood meeting, or was Mary Magdalene out collecting contributions for a Lottie Moon offering?"

As for his methods and the resulting publicity, those who can attest for positive results from Harrington in-

Jack Allen, barber in the House of Representatives, gives a copy of Bob's "Wake Up, America!" message to Melvin Laird, Secretary of Defense.

Is There Room for Non-Conformists? —{63}—

clude such leading New Orleans Baptists as J. D. Grey, pastor of the First Church, a staunch supporter of Harrington's ministry, and H. Leo Eddleman, president of New Orleans Seminary, who issued the challenge which Harrington accepted when he began his unorthodox endeavor.

Included in these results is Harrington's claim of converting Carlos Marcello, internationally-known racketeer; a night club owner's conversion, along with a host of lesser known characters who are often referred to as "riff-raff"; and an awareness of God in what has often been considered one of the nation's most cancerous pockets of vice and corruption with charges ranging from white slavery to open narcotics traffic.

Harrington, whose red tie, handkerchief and socks are a personal trademark, is a colorful personality, but not one without enemies, such as an anonymous Mobile, Ala., woman who wrote a letter in which she said, "You are making a mockery of the Lord. I have started praying today for you to die."

Bob has a deep sense of patriotism.

(PAGE 65) Jerry Falwell, Lynchburg, Virginia and Bob view destruction caused by Hurricane Camille.

Brother Bob, as some of New Orleans' uptown skeptics call him, also has a knack for having some fellow Baptists as potential adversaries.

This is the same man who has won the respect (according to candid observation) of the entertainers and barkers along Bourbon Street for his sincere efforts to win souls for Christ. A few holdouts, especially among the entertainers, mostly women, are still skeptics.

Harrington is the first to say that every one of his skeptics is eagerly waiting for him to either make a misstep or to "put in a commercial gimmick." Says Harrington, "The minute that it appears that this is a venture for making money, my work is dead here."

Unfortunately, many of his skeptics are not "riff-raff," but are bona fide church-goers, he states, rebuking him for daring to preach the Gospel where he says it is needed most.

According to the evangelist, who is also busy in conducting revivals and crusades, he got the inspiration to

Is There Room for Non-Conformists? ---❦{65}❦---

"set up shop" on Bourbon Street from Leo Eddleman, when the seminary president challenged seminarians with this statement: "Wherever there's a pocket of sin, it is a mission field and the nearest Christian to it is a missionary."

Harrington's self-admitted philosophy before he was "reborn" in 1958 was "anything goes, so long as my wife and my pastor don't find out."

Then a Methodist layman and an insurance agent in Alabama, Harrington decided to give his all to the Gospel ministry. While a seminarian, he was chosen by J. D. Grey to become assistant pastor at New Orleans' First church. He has credited Grey with inspiration in his endeavors, along with his wife, a private school teacher, and a handful of financial supporters who had enough confidence in his methods to get him started.

Harrington's down-to-earth style of preaching, his ability to parry sarcasm with quick, clean wit, and his ever-present aura of joy in his endeavors have won him many

Bob with Dr. T. A. Patterson, Executive Secretary, Texas Baptists

God's Super Salesman

friends away from Bourbon Street. Already known throughout New Orleans, he believes in exposure so that those seeking spiritual and moral support know where to get in touch with him. One way he has attempted to do this is by placing a huge billboard ad on the corner of Canal and Royal in the heart of New Orleans' business district. The $1,000 tab for this venture is being shared by a group of laymen familiar with advertising.

Self-publicity is not his goal, he claims, stating, "If I had started this venture here for the purpose of merely getting publicity, I wouldn't have gotten any of the results which have come from it."

Among the humorous aspects of his unique ministry have been the "closing down of his 'church' by District Attorney Jim Garrison" when Garrison shuttered the Circus Club on Bourbon Street; a request from the proprietor of an alleged house of ill repute for him to turn off his loudspeaker and sacred music "because it was running the customers away," and a situation where a drunk came to him after listening to a 45-minute long sermon, asking Harrington for a "quarter to buy a bottle of beer."

. . . .

This then is a non-conformist Baptist preacher, shunned by some, envied by others.

In Harrington's own words, "I don't restrict myself to the limitations of the normal clergyman, so I must be considered a non-conformist. However, when you get right down to it, the greatest non-conformist in the history of the world was Jesus Christ. There is a lot of room for more non-conformists in this world," he said.

10. Be a Disturber of the Peace

Don't be afraid to rock the boat, that is if Christ is your pilot. Don't be afraid of change if it is for the better. Don't be afraid of the unusual. Anyone who has done anything outstanding, or is doing something outstanding, is usually doing the unusual, and somebody is being disturbed. Be very sure when you shoot your cannon that you know your target and have abundant ammunition, then let go. Remember, you will never know the full potential of your project until you, by faith, give it the works.

Jesus, the greatest sales manager, said in Matthew 10: 34–36, "Think not that I am come to send peace on earth: I came not to send peace, but a sword. For I am come to set a man at variance against his father, and the daughter against her mother, and the daughter in law against her mother in law. And a man's foes shall be they of his own household."

On April 15, 1958 when Christ became my Lord and personal Saviour I immediately became a disturber of the peace. First I disturbed the self-righteous peace in the families of my loved ones. I rocked my mother's religious boat, and she became my first convert. My mother was as church-centered as possible, but lost without Christ until Christ through me disturbed the peace. The same is true for my daddy, active in churchianity, but without Christ. Fifteen days later his boat was shook, and he saw himself as a sinner going to hell without Christ, and he got saved. My daddy surrendered to preach

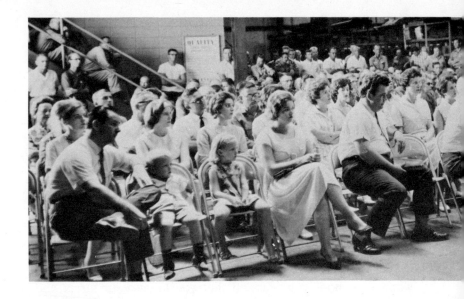

in his late 50's, and he now serves as a Methodist church pastor.

Oh, how my Lord helped me to disturb the peace in my own immediate family! My wife wanted me to get religion, but not like I got it. Three days after my conversion I went to preaching, and my wife went home to her mother for advice and strength. It took a few months for the boat to settle down, but then she realized Jesus was my pilot and would be ours. Since this, the sailing has been much better.

Here's a great sermon outline on "Disturber of the Peace." Preach and practice it!

Text: *Matthew 10:34–36 "Think not that I am come to send peace on earth: I came not to send peace, but a sword. For I am come to set a man at variance against his father, and the daughter against her mother, and the daughter in law against her mother in law. And a man's foes shall be they of his own household."*

Who needs to be disturbed? You and I do—

Employees of the Taylor Machine Works plant in Louisville, Mississippi hear Bob.

1st: *The Pastor:* "Shepherd of the flock!"
  A. About the spiritual condition of the church
     (1) Worldliness—within and without
  B. The lost people in his church field.
  C. The growth of the saints in the church.
2nd: The Deacons: Disturbed over his calling.
  (Servant—not dictator) helper not ruler
     Illustration: There must be a special hot corner in Hell for the Judas type Deacon, griping, complaining. Don't put that oil on Jesus—let's use the money.
     1 Timothy 3:4: "One that ruleth well his own household, having his children in subjection with all gravity."
     "Being found blameless"—Who? You could if you would!
     Deacon should be disturbed over not winning souls to Jesus.
3rd. The Superintendents:
  Disturbed over their
     (1) Department

      (2) Visitation

      (3) Grades

      (4) Spiritual life

4th: The Teachers:

Disturbed over their

      (1) Class

      (2) Fellowship

      (3) Lost souls

      (4) Prayer life

5th: Church Member:

Disturbed over:

      (1) Lost or Saved

      (2) Happy or unhappy

      (3) Fruitful

      (4) What's first place

NOW—ACT—NOW!

"All of 'em
tune in to Bob."

Young and old alike turn on with **Bob's** preaching.

11. Get Attention to Your Witness

I believe in using everything you can that will bring glory to God in getting attention to your witness for Christ. One idea my Lord gave me soon after my conversion was the red tie, red handkerchief, and red socks as a personal trademark. Not only is red a good attention-getting color, but it also can represent the blood of Jesus shed on Calvary for the remission of our sins. This trademark has become very famous, and I want to share a photograph with a news article concerning my official tie maker, Mrs. Jay Hatcher of Milan, Tennessee.

He'll Greet President Nixon
In A Red, Made-In-Milan Tie

When one of the South's most noted Baptist ministers speaks at services in the White House next month, he'll be wearing a special red tie that was hand-made in Milan.

Bro. Bob Harrington, known nation-wide as the Chaplain of Bourbon Street, had a problem in obtaining the now-fashionable wide ties in bright red which are his trademark, along with red handkerchief and red socks. But while in Milan last week conducting a revival, he confided in Mrs. Jay Hatcher and solved his problem.

But it wasn't all that simple. Mrs. Hatcher, though owner of a fabric shop here for 12 years, had never constructed a tie before. And it's almost by accident that she's making them now.

"Bro. Bob dropped by the shop for coffee last week and in discussing his dilemma, he asked me if I could make him some wide ties," Mrs. Hatcher said. "He had shopped almost everywhere but was unable to find red ties that are as wide as the present fashion."

Mrs. Hatcher agreed to try it and went to work.

(Reprinted from the *Milan* (Tennessee) *Mirror,* January 30, 1969. Used by permission.)

Mrs. Hatcher "borrowed" one of my regular ties, ripped it apart, and used it as a pattern for ties she makes me out of red wrinkle-proof satin. I've designated her my "Official Tie Maker."

Do these ties draw attention to my witness?

They certainly do!

Mrs. Jay Hatcher, Colonial Fabric Shops, Milan, Tennessee is Bob's official red tie and handkerchief maker.

Bob has been on many
TV shows. Here he
talks with Dennis Wholley,
Cincinnati, Ohio.

12. Satan Brings Happiness

"Satan Brings Happiness" is the name of the most popular tract we pass out on Bourbon Street. This is quite startling to any person—especially someone who might think Satan really brings happiness. Note the reverse approach, the indirect way of getting across a direct message.

"Satan Brings Happiness"

Don't let anybody kid you. You can be happy in Satan, but you really have to concentrate.

Forget about the TEN COMMANDMENTS! With Satan as your god these commandments do not apply. You can kill, steal, commit adultery, lie, curse, envy, and ignore your parents.

Forget about LAW ENFORCEMENT AGENTS! Ignore policemen. Curse them. Spit at them. Throw beer bottles at them. With Satan as your protector you don't need policemen.

Forget about TRAFFIC LAWS! Jay-walk. Lie down in front of traffic. Drive through red lights. Plow through "Don't Enter" signs on one-way streets. Satan is now your god. He opposes restrictions.

Forget about HEALTH! Express yourself fully. Live fast. Ride the needle. Smoke several packs a day. Flip

Brother Bob counseling with a troubled young woman

(BELOW) A serious moment in the presentation of the gospel

pills. Pop Bottles. Travel on LSD. Don't sleep. Stay on the move. Satan promotes fast living.

Forget about FRIENDS and FAMILY! Bring your wife, sisters, and daughters to Bourbon Street. Make strip-teasers out of them. After the shows, sell them as prostitutes. After all, if someone else hadn't brought his wife, daughters, and sisters you couldn't lust over the current belles.

Forget about CALVARY! Ignore that God loves you and gave his Son to die for you. Ignore that God sent not his Son into the world to condemn you but that you, through him, might be saved.

FURTHERMORE—

Don't die, because you are going to hell. "The wages of

Typical of
Harrington's ministry

(BELOW) A witness to those not
ordinarily found in churches.

sin is death." You are just one heartbeat from hell. Be careful.

Don't break down your body, because venereal diseases, lung cancer, and alcoholism are hard to cure.

Don't run out of money, because Satan can make you happy only so long as you have rolls of money to spend. Don't expect to hold a good-paying job, because Satan's marks disqualify you.

Don't cry out for help, because Satan has no time to help his foolish victims.

Face reality, because the Bible warns: "Sin brings pleasure just for a season." You will harvest what you plant. Give your heart to Jesus and let Him guide your life. Jesus said: "I am the way, the truth, and the LIFE.

I came that you might have life more abundantly." Jesus brings real Happiness.

HOW DO YOU ACCEPT JESUS?

"Except ye repent, ye shall all likewise perish" (Luke 13:5).

"Believe on the Lord Jesus Christ, and thou shalt be saved" (Acts 16:31).

NOW: More about our enemy—*Satan.*

Satan is one of the numerous names given to the Evil Spirit, who rules the kingdom of darkness. It means adversary and designates him as the opposer of all that is good and all who desire or strive to be good.

He is more commonly called the devil (Greek *diabolos,* false-accuser) and is the chief spirit in the realm of evil.

Bob's endeavor is to witness anywhere there is a need for Christ.

The Bible designates Satan as a person by personal names, personal pronouns, personal acts. He has a personal career and a definite personal conflict and overthrow.

Satan has many names: Satan, Job 1:6, Luke 10:18; devil, Matthew 4:1; Abaddon, Revelation 9:11; Beelzebub, Matthew 12:24; Belial, 2 Corinthians 6:15; Adversary, 1 Peter 5:8; Dragon, Revelation 12; Serpent, Genesis 3, Revelation 12.

HE IS A VERY GREAT PERSON. He could contend with Michael the Archangel, Jude 9. He accomplished the entrance of sin and fall of man, Genesis 3. He can appear before God, Job 1:6, 2:1. He walketh about like a roaring lion, 1 Peter 5:8. He deceiveth the nations, Revelation 12:9, 20:3. He is the accuser in heaven, Revelation 12:10. He holdeth the whole world like children asleep in his arms, 1 John 5:19, Matthew 13:38. He has the power of death, Hebrews 2:14.

The notion that Satan has already been cast out and is now confined in hell (Hades) is founded on a wrong conception of Luke 10:18 and Revelation 12. Doth are prophetic language, and refer to a future event. Satan still has access to the heavens as in the days of Job (1:6; 2:1) and is there "as the accuser of the brethren" (Rev. 12:10). He is still "the prince of the power of the air" (Eph. 2:2), and he is "the god of this world" (2 Cor. 4:4).

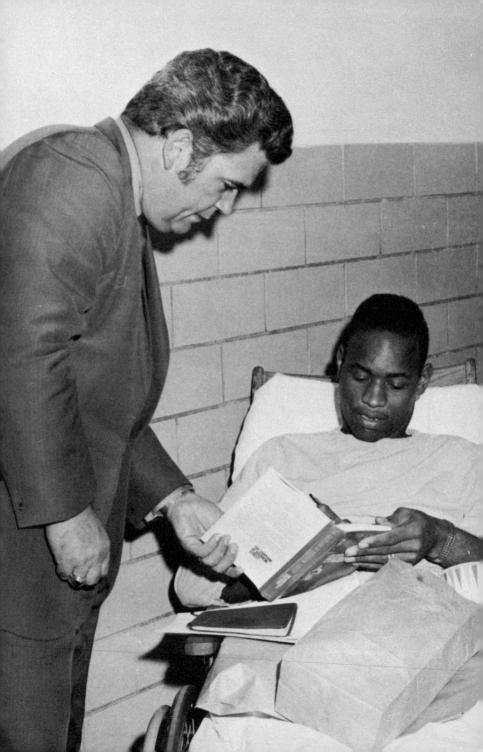

13. Cold Calls for Christ

One of the most difficult obstacles for me to over-come when I first went to work for Liberty National Life Insurance Company as a debit salesman was the making of "cold calls." I believe this is a big hold-back among Christian witnessing today. How to begin? How to knock on that strange door, not sure who is on the other side. How to approach a stranger with a witness for Christ. Many times I have gone visiting in the name of Christ and prayed for the leadership of the Holy Spirit and approached a house, knocked on the door and prayed that no one would be at home. Haven't you?

Charlie Clay, my first superintendent, who introduced me to the insurance business, was the one man who taught me how to make effective cold calls and come away with a sale. The Agent's Training School my company sent me to was also most helpful, but the one thing that did it for me was my actual do-ing it for myself. As I write this article the index finger knuckles on both my hands twelve years later still show the result of door knocking and cold-calling!

I subscribe to "Salesman's Workshop," published by Bureau of Business Practice of Waterford, Connecticut, and each month I get lessons on many sales ideas, many of which I can apply to my Christian witnessing. One booklet was sent me called "Cold-Call Selling." May I share with you some of the good ideas I received from this booklet?

The first secret of cold-call selling is the right attitude. "A man's success in selling (witnessing) is dependent more on his mental attitude than on his ability. There are more salesmen who fear they will lose a sale than there are those who are

Bob visits Printers Alley in Nashville, Tennessee to witness for Christ.

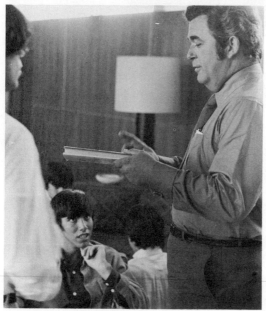

Sometimes an entire story can be told in a single individual's eyes.

confident of winning out." Consider your attitude toward the prospect. It's all too easy to knock on a door without giving any prior thought to the people inside. Some salesmen (visiting for Christ and the Church) consider these people as names . . . not prospects. The salesman who uses cold-call canvassing most successfully is the man who is genuinely concerned about people. He knows in advance that the prospect needs his service. He has enough respect for his product so that he isn't willing to take a fast "no" for an answer without asking the prospect why. He also has enough respect for himself so that he is sure of his position . . . sure that he can help the prospect solve his problem. He believes very strongly that everybody is a prospect until proved otherwise.

The second secret of cold-call selling is planning. Yes, there is such a thing as planning your cold-calls! The right kind of planning will pay off in dollars and cents (souls saved, additions to your church, growth, you name it). Now, plan your work and work your plans.

14. Thank God I've Found Me!

Do you know who you are?

Where you are going?

And what you are doing?

I personally doubt if you can be of any spiritual help to anyone unless you have found out this information concerning yourself.

Many times before my conversion to Christ and his way of living I sought out guidance from others, but to no avail. For example: my wife suggested that I visit a domestic court judge to find out how we might save our marriage. I made an appointment with this particular judge in Mobile County. He said to me, "Mr. Harrington, what seems to be your problem?" In all sincerity I told him, "I don't know, Judge." This is TRUE. I didn't know I was a lost, hell-bound sinner, living for the devil and myself. I had never been told that I needed to repent of my sins and trust Christ to save my soul.

Then the judge said, "Well, what are you doing that your wife disapproves of?" In the best way I knew how I stated: "I smoke, drink, party, run around a little, stay out late a little, etc." Then the judge looked me straight in the eye and said, "Is this all that you're doing, Mr. Harrington?" I said, "Yes." The judge quickly added, "I can't help you, man. If I could, I'd help myself." This I believe is one of the reasons for so much confusion and unrest in our sin-sick society today. You have the blind leading the blind and they both end up in the ditch. Now the ditch is so crowded it has taken on the

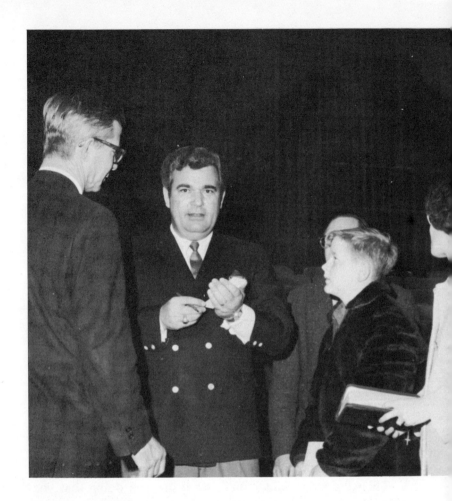

status symbol.

Thank God for the night of April 15, 1958 when I, for the first time in my thirty years of living (existing), while visiting the Sweet Water Baptist Church looking for life insurance prospects, saw myself. The Holy Spirit of God pulled the curtains back and showed me ME. I was ugly. I was a hypocrite. I was two-faced. I was a failure as a husband, daddy, and man. It was a horrible but real picture of me. Thank God I found me. The precious Holy Spirit not only brought me under powerful conviction, but he also prepared the way for me to invite Christ into my heart as my personal Saviour, Lord, and Master.

Remember, it's not a pretty picture to find yourself through God's eyes, but you will never truly repent and be saved until you do.

Thank God I found out that John 3:16 was meant for me personally. Thank God I found out I was a lost sinner, playing church on the road to Hell. Thank God I found out "Jesus loves Me." Thank God I found out what even Nicodemus didn't know . . . how to be born-again.

Thank God I found out we can be saved by faith in Jesus Christ through the grace of God the Father, and it's not reforming, turning over new leaves, or making new resolutions. I heard Evangelist Angel Martinez say one night in our church during revival a few years after my conversion: "Reformation is what we do for God. Regeneration is what God does for us."

Thank God I've found me. *Have you? Really?*

15. Your Sin Will Find You Out

As a preacher I'm prone to preach to others: "Your sin will find you out." Quickly adding: "The Bible states in Romans 6:23, "The wages of sin is death." BUT, as I look and read Romans closer I find out Paul is telling this to the saints (saved) at Rome. Now, I add to my preaching: "My sin will find me out." Ouch, this hurts. In pointing my index finger at you and your sin I notice on closer examination that I have three other fingers pointing back at me.

The most horrible thing about sin is that it is so universally and inescapably deadly. It kills, without regard of person or position! It kills the young. It destroys the old. There is nothing holy for it. There is nothing sacred to it. Satan and sin encroach into the very sanctities of life, staining them with their slimy trails. That the wages of sin is death is recognized throughout the world. That the soul that sinneth must face punishment and eternal condemnation is written in the warp and woof of all mankind, civilized and uncivilized, Christian and unbelieving. Eternal punishment, the flaming torments of hell, were originally, according to God's Word, prepared for the devil and his angels. Since then, however, hell has become peopled and is still being filled with the gainsayers, the unbelieving, the overt transgressors of God's laws and requirements.

Sin is laborious, spending for things that will perish with using. When we get it, what do we have? We have to leave it all behind. It turns to ashes, to gall, to bitter wormwood. Go

(RIGHT)
Harrington in action
on Bourbon Street
(Home Board photo)

(BELOW) Harrington
is at home with a
microphone in his hands.

out into the highways and byways of life. Watch the faces of
the devotees of Satan. See how strained they are. See what
efforts they put forth in order to obtain the things of this
world, when in their sober moments they know that everything
they do get will result in their harm, in their loss, in their spiritual death. The way of the transgressor is hard. The wicked
are like the troubled sea. The devil has no bargains. You pay
a thousand times over for every bauble that you obtain in his
marketplace. He cannot even give you a deed in fee simple.
He has no control over life, over death, over eternity. Only
God has that.

Sin is costly, more costly than any and every other pursuit,
more expensive than any and every other engagement of life.
It costs everything—character, influence, reputation, time,

**Harrington is a
fiery pulpiteer.**

health, love, home, money. Finally, it costs the soul and heaven itself. "For what shall it profit a man if he gain the whole world and lose his own soul?" On top of that, you must remember—oh! I beseech you to remember—that the devil cannot, that the Devil does not, that the devil will not ever give anyone the whole world in exchange for his soul. He bought Judas for thirty pieces of silver. Before that time and since he has been buying the eternal welfare of mankind, sometimes for even less than that. Examine what the devil has to offer you and you will find that it is shoddy, that there is nothing to it, that it is not even worth one millionth of the price that the devil asks for it, that it is painted up and perfumed over to make it attractive, that there is nothing solid about it.

Sin is extremely unsatisfying. There is nothing in sin that contents for any length of time. It is bitter, biting, blighting. It blights like the burning furnace, like the blazing noontide heat. It brings pains to the body, pangs to the heart, punishment to the soul. It is a whip of scorpions by day, a nightmare by night, the shadow of an inevitable doom hanging like the

Your Sin Will Find You Out —⋙{97}⋘—

sword of Damocles over the head of the sinner. You lose yourself for awhile in its hectic preoccupation, but as soon as the moments of enchantment are over, there comes the bitter sting of repentance, of remorse, of biting memories.

In one of my revival messages I take my text from Numbers 32:23, "But if ye will not do so, behold, ye have sinned against the Lord; and be sure your sin will find you out."

Sin has no respect of person nor denomination.

In the above text Moses was trying to get the Reubenites to put God first as I am attempting to do in my "Wake Up America" crusade to get our 200 million Americans to put God first in their lives.

Your sin will find you out in:

Friendliness wins many.

First, your face
Second, your body
Third, your character
Fourth, your conscience
Fifth, your children
Sixth, in open public shame
Seventh, in judgment and hell

Not only will sin find us out individually, but collectively as a family, home and nation.

Remember as you live, that the last part of Romans 6:23 tells us ". . . but, the gift of God is eternal life through Jesus Christ our Lord."

Jesus paid it all
All to him I owe.
Sin has left a crimson stain—
But his blood washed it white as snow.

Student response
to Harrington is
very good.

Have you heard him?
Bob Harrington
America's Dynamic Preacher
BIG TENT
REVIVAL
Nightly 7:30 PM
900 E. Main St.
Sponsored by
Grandview Baptist Church

16. Bob's Bad on Booze

Every man and woman who makes a living from the booze industry is a parasite. This goes for the fellow

Who voted to repeal the eighteenth amendment,
The man who issued the license,
The man who rents the building,
The man who drives the truck that hauls it,
And the man, or even the beautiful young girl, who slides the stuff across the counter.

THEY ARE ALL IN THE SAME CATEGORY!

Booze has:

Made more orphans,
Taken bread out of more babies' mouths,
Taken more shoes off more babies' feet,
Taken the roses out of precious mothers' cheeks,
Caused more tears to flow from eyes,
Dug more graves,
Broken up more homes,
Led to more pre-marital sex relations

THAN ANY OTHER ONE THING KNOWN TO THE HUMAN RACE!

Nothing good can be said about it! It's a killer! It's a parasite! It's a liar! It's a sneak! It's a subtle serpent! It knows no exceptions; it is no respecter of persons. It is still the same sneaking, subtle, slimy slop it has always been—whether in a honky-tonk, country club, or your own personal padded bar in your house (not *home,* a *home* would not have a booze bar).

We spend millions and millions of dollars every year to chase down and convict criminals, and we have Public Enemy Number One (booze) residing on our public squares.

By the way, how long has it been since you have heard a good red-hot sermon in your church on booze?

The Bible says: "Cry aloud against the sins of the people." "Reprove, rebuke!"

While liquor and beer are on the main streets of our cities every boy and girl is in danger.

As the spider to the bug,

As the hawk to the little innocent biddy,

As the mad dog to the little innocent child,

So is booze to the entire human race—the rich, the poor, the young, the old, the white, the black. It excludes no one and includes everyone.

Shame, disgrace, reproach, indecency, immorality—these are the words always connected with drink. There are forty million or more drinkers of booze in America. Drinking is a short cut to hell—if you are in a hurry to get there.

My good friend Evangelist Oliver Greene of Radio's Gospel Hour holds no punches when it comes to battling booze. Some of these quotes come from Brother Greene's writings. Thank you, Oliver, and keep socking it to the devil and his crowd.

> When a man is drunk, he is beastly! He bleats and babbles like a goat. He lays in the gutter like a hog!

"One evening in October
When I was far from sober
And dragging home a load with manly pride,
My feet began to stutter,
So I lay down in the gutter,
And a pig came up and parked right by my side.
Then I warbled, it's fair weather
When good fellows get together;
Till a lady passing by was heard to say:
'You can tell a man who boozes
By the company he chooses,'
THEN THE PIG GOT UP AND SLOWLY WALKED AWAY."

Mr. Preacher, Deacon, professional worker for Christ, "Take a strong stand, man, or resign."

It will be most interesting at judgment to witness what will happen to many of these so-called Christian laymen who serve as deacons, stewards, and elders (also on Christian college boards and seminary developments) who are such big givers to the Lord's work and much of their profit coming from the sales of booze or renting property to those who make it and sell it.

College students listen to the gospel.

The Drunkard's Twenty-Third Psalm:

King Alcohol is my shepherd: I shall always want.
He maketh me to lie down in the gutters,
He leadeth me beside troubled waters,
He destroyeth my soul,
He leadeth me into the paths of wickedness for the effects
    sake,
Yea, though I walk through the valley of poverty and
    have delirium tremens,
I will cling to drink.
For thou art with me, thy bite and thy sting they torment
    me.

Harrington
preaches on campus.

Thou preparest an empty table before me in the presence
    of my family,
Thou anointest my head with hellishness,
My cup of wrath runneth over.
Surely destruction and misery shall follow me all of my
    life,
And I shall dwell in the house of the damned forever!

JESUS SAID:
"Go ye into all
the world and
preach the Gospel..."
MARK 16:15

17. Check'em Out

In my life insurance selling days for Liberty National and Pan-American I believed everybody who could breathe was a prospect until proven otherwise by checking him out. I have carried this same rule into my work as an evangelist to preach the gospel to every creature. Everyone I come in contact with is a prospect for my Christ, and I check them out. This started with my conversion on April 15, 1958. I try to check out at least one person each day in my daily routine of home, office, and travel. The more you check-'em out the easier it becomes. "Was it ever difficult?" you ask. "Yes, it was in the beginning and during the formative years while developing muscles in my soul." It still gets difficult if you let much time or many days come between your checking-'em out experiences. Keep faithful in your check-'em out ministry. Don't ever presume someone to be saved; check him out!

Paul, the apostle was a check-'em out expert. He didn't let anyone by from kings to jailers. Paul was faithful unto death with checking out sinners. In Acts 19:2, Paul walked up outside a local church at Ephesus, probably between Sunday School hour and the morning service, finding some of the members, some deacons and general church officers, and said to them, "Have ye received the Holy Ghost since ye believed? And they said unto him, We have not so much as heard whether there be any Holy Ghost." By this bold check-'em out conviction, Paul led twelve to Christ. The Bible doesn't say if there were more than twelve, but there may have been some typical churchite who became offended by Paul's bold witness. I have offended some with my boldness in checking-'em out for Christ. I remember a few weeks after my conversion I joined the First Baptist Church of Chickasaw, Alabama, where Dr. Bob Barker is the fine pastor. I checked out the staff, the deacons, and everybody. I didn't know any better. I thought saved people would appreciate it, but oh, did I find out different. One night after prayer meeting I went over to a group of ladies in our church. I was excited over being saved, and prayer meeting had just turned me on. I looked at this one rather stout lady and said, "Mam, are you saved?" Maybe I was too happy when I asked her, and she must have thought I was being funny because she looked at me with fire in her eyes and

At the cross . . .

spouted, "I'll have you to know I was a Christian a long time before you were, Mr. Harrington." This woman was so mad at me for checking her out that she could have killed me. That night I prayed for her husband because he has to live with that thorn (or horn) in the flesh.

Thank God all I check out don't react as this woman did. Most are thankful I cared enough to be concerned about them.

May I share my ABC's of checking-'em out?

A = All are lost without Christ.
    All have sinned (Rom. 3:23)
    Any time is a good time to check-'em out.

B = Believe that Jesus can save.
    Be prepared always to check-'em out.
    Be prayed up and ready.
    Blood of Jesus can wash away sins.

C = Christ is the answer.
    Christ can change a sinner.
    Come to Jesus.
    Call upon Christ, and he will hear.

Check-'em out! Remember the only person our Lord calls wise in his Word is "He that winneth souls." You can't win the lost to Christ unless you "check-'em out."

18. I Met the Chaplain of Bourbon Street

While in CBS-City, Hollywood, California to video-tape my second appearance on Art Linkletter's House Party, I was introduced to one of Mr. Linkletter's writers, Walter Wagner. Mr. Wagner was to glean from me information so as to compile material for Art to ask me questions on his show. *Christian Life* magazine published what happened by the man it happened to. Here it is (reprinted by permission):

I Met "the Chaplain of Bourbon Street"

By Walter Wagner

"The bright lights from the make-up mirrors cast shadows across evangelist Bob Harrington's face as he leaned against a dressing table and talked quietly with a stripper in a small room backstage at a New Orleans' Bourbon Street night club. Blaring rhythms could be heard through the thin walls while "The Chaplain of Bourbon Street" made the girl face the question of whether she wanted to spend eternity in heaven or hell.

No one except Harrington is permitted in the dressing rooms of the strippers, but I was allowed to accompany him on this humid summer night. His object: to interview one of the girls. She was a raven-haired beauty, only 18, who had been taking off her clothes for pay for more than a year. Starting as a go-go dancer in Washington, D.C., she had come to New Orleans to be with her boyfriend, who was studying at Tulane. Stripping was the only way she could earn a living, she said.

Harrington does not try to convert Bourbon Street sinners by dragging them kicking and screaming into a highsteepled, air-conditioned church with cushioned pews. He talked softly but directly, and the girl admitted she was not happy in her job. She had to fend off both lecherous men and lesbians. She had been offered marijuana, heroin and LSD more times than she could count. As we left she promised to visit Harrington's office the next day. She did—and he brought her to the Lord.

"Watch for that big fellow with the red Bible," one Bourbon Street club owner warned his barker. "He's going to convert all our strippers." When the barker told Harrington he had orders to keep him out, the Chaplain barged inside and told the proprietor, "Don't worry about my converting all your strippers. If I do, you'll have a new batch tomorrow." The owner smiled—and never again denied Harrington admittance to his premises.

I had known little about this unusual preacher from New Orleans until July 17, 1967 when he came into my life with shattering impact. I was a writer for Art Linkletter's "House Party" television show, and I had been assigned to pre-interview Harrington in preparation for his appearance on the program.

I approached the assignment as routine. In ten years as a writer on the show, I had interviewed thousands of people—virtually every movie and television personality in Hollywood, governors, mayors, even the Shah of Iran —big people, important people as well as people who had flashed into the headlines for a brief moment of glory,

then disappeared again into anonymity. I had also once interviewed evangelist Billy Graham, who had made an enormously favorable impression on me.

So, as I waited for Bob Harrington that morning, I was not impressed, nor did it occur to me that my meeting with him would change my life.

He arrived promptly at ten a.m., a smiling, 240-pound, six-footer wearing red accessories—tie, pocket handkerchief and socks. Under his arm he carried a blood-red Bible.

"I want the sinners to see me coming," he said when I asked why he dressed so flamboyantly.

We sat down in my small office and Harrington began to talk of his ministry—his work on Bourbon Street with strippers, prostitutes, homosexuals, alcoholics, pimps, barkers and drug addicts.

The stories he told me were almost unbelievable. I thought of myself as a sophisticated, somewhat cynical

**Bob with
Dr. Foy Valentine
and Rev. John Bisagno**

Hollywood writer who had seen and heard everything. But Harrington was taking me into a world completely alien to my previous experience and starting me on a journey I never thought I was capable of making. He talked convincingly of the saving power of Christ, how the anguish and emotional instability of millions of Americans was caused by a separation from the Lord.

We polished off the interview quickly. On two three-by-five index cards I wrote suggested questions for Linkletter and indicated what Harrington's answers would be. The interview was to last about eight minutes and I could only skim the cream. There was far more to Harrington than could be encompassed in the rigid time demands of a television interview.

I had felt an unexpected rapport with Harrington. And while we waited for him to make his appearance on the show at 11:30, I found myself telling him about my personal life, secrets I had done my best to hide from my associates.

I told him that two years before I had taken an evening walk to buy a newspaper. By the time I returned home I was breathing with extreme difficulty (hyper-ventilation was the medical term for it, I later discovered). When my wife saw me gasping for breath, she phoned our family doctor. We both thought I was having a heart attack.

At nine o'clock that evening the doctor met us at his office. He examined me and said there was nothing physically wrong. Perhaps, he suggested, I had been working too hard. "You're in a high-tension profession. Slow down and relax. If the symptoms persist, I'll prescribe a tranquilizer."

The condition did persist. Three weeks later the breathing difficulty returned, accompanied by worse symptoms —blinding dizziness, sweating palms, a weird feeling in my stomach. I felt that I was going to faint at any moment.

I returned to the doctor. He could still find no physical cause for my symptoms. He said that the symptoms probably were psychological and advised me to enter a sanitarium for a complete physical and emotional check-up.

I was in the sanitarium a month. My world had suddenly caved in, and I could not understand why. I was earning $25,000 a year, living in an $80,000 home, had a lovely wife and two beautiful young daughters. By all the standards of the American dream, I was a success and had a future brimming with promise.

After an exhaustive physical examination I was given a clean bill of health. Yet the symptoms were still there. In fact, they were growing worse day by day.

I was introduced to the hospital's chief psychiatrist. A pleasant, dedicated man, he visited me every morning at nine a.m. We talked of my background, of my Jewish upbringing and how I had abandoned my religion years before as irrelevant. We discussed my childhood and my relationships with my parents and friends. We dissected my family life.

"You need therapy," the psychiatrist told me, "deep personal therapy."

I was aghast. It couldn't be happening. The world of the mentally ill was as foreign to me as the control panel on a spaceship.

"How long will the therapy take?" I asked.

"The question is not how long it will take, but how we can make you a happier, more mature person."

"But what's wrong with me?"

"You're suffering from extreme anxiety symptoms," the psychiatrist said.

That was a polite way of saying I was in the throes of a complete nervous breakdown.

After my discharge from the hospital I began having private therapy twice a week.

I went back to my job, but I wasn't making it because the symptoms were worse than ever. One morning the dizziness and the rumblings in my stomach were so bad that I had to leave the studio early, after barely completing my work. I went home and fell into bed—scared, confused, my emotions completely out of control.

At my next meeting with my psychiatrist I told him I had fallen apart on the job. He put me on a heavy diet of tranquilizers—six a day, one Meprobamate and Stelazine when I awoke, another Meprobamate at two p.m., a Librium at five p.m., a Nembutal to help me sleep.

The tranquilizers barely managed to hold me together, and in panic I talked to my therapist about these strange new feelings. He told me that I had been suppressing my anger all my life and now it was coming out in ways that could be lethal.

"You must struggle at all times to maintain conscious control of your behavior," he advised. I did the best I could—and thank God I didn't kill anyone.

But the deeper I plunged into psychiatry, the less effect it had on me. My work began to suffer. I was lost and helpless, barely managing to hang on day after day. Seeing no hope for a cure I considered suicide.

All this I confided to Harrington. "You need the Lord," he said. "Christ is your answer."

"Two years of psychiatry haven't helped," I protested. "What can the Lord do for me?"

"The best psychiatrist in the world is Christ," Harrington answered.

Before I could protest, Harrington got up and closed the door to my small backstage office. While stage-hands, grips, cameramen, cable-haulers, the hundred or so behind-the-scenes people it takes to put on a television show milled around, Harrington put his hand on my shoulder and said, "Let's pray."

"I don't know how," I answered, afraid of what was coming yet yearning to meet God through this evangelist I had met only an hour before.

Harrington began praying, and he asked me to repeat each line of the invitation to come to God. He asked God to forgive my sins and bring tranquility into the life of a troubled soul.

The prayer lasted only a few moments. But it had a powerful effect on me. Suddenly I felt cleansed and inspired. The more I thought about my dramatic, totally unanticipated acceptance of God, the more confident I became. Some of my fear began to ebb away. For the first time since my breakdown, I experienced a moment of tranquility. I put everything in God's hands, my survival, my destiny, and, hopefully, a new serenity.

At 11:30 Harrington walked out on stage for his interview with Linkletter. The Chaplain of Bourbon Street held the audience spellbound. He was alternately witty and profound as he told the story of how he set up shop as an uninvited soul-saver on the most sin-soaked street in America. He gave an account of how hostile nightclub owners had hired a stripper to compromise him and thus discredit him as an opportunistic Elmer Gantry. Cheers and applause rang through the studio at the conclusion of his interview. Subsequently, Harrington's appearance drew more mail than any guest who had appeared on our show during the year. Our office switchboard lit up with inquiries from people wanting to know more about Harrington.

Immediately after the program dozens of people from the studio audience ignored the commands of network ushers that no unauthorized persons were permitted backstage and made their way to Harrington. He was bombarded with questions, congratulated and plied with requests for autographs.

Harrington had struck a chord in me. He had had the same effect on the audience.

I was dazzled by his power. When the last admirer finally wandered off, Harrington and I were alone.

"More people should know about your work," I said. "Have you thought of writing a book?"

Harrington laughed, and in his soft Alabama drawl, he said, "Now I know the Lord brought us together."

From his briefcase he extracted a sheaf of notes. "I've been wanting to write a book for years and here's some material. Why don't you write the book with me?"

I told him there was nothing I would rather do.

I immediately called my editor at Doubleday, Richard Laughran, and told him I had found a man whose experiences would electrify America and that a book about him was a natural.

Harrington was due to fly back to New Orleans in a few hours. Dick hurried out to the airport to meet him. He was immediately as enthusiastic as I about a book on Harrington.

Brother
Bob's Buddies

In a few weeks the firm's publishing committee approved the project, and I was soon on my way to New Orleans to gather the necessary background on Harrington. Meanwhile, I had begun tapering off on my tranquilizers. I was down to three a day and was seeing my psychiatrist less often. The freedom from fear through my new reliance on God, generated by Harrington, was working.

I had never imagined what New Orleans was really like. I had spent five years in Europe and had seen the worst fleshpots of Paris, Hamburg and Naples. New Orleans easily outdistanced them all as a sinkhole of sin.

With Harrington, I strolled through the tough, wretched French Quarter. I found Bourbon Street a street where anything can be had for a price—a fix, a girl, a boy, a stag movie.

Strippers bump and grind through the night in simulated paroxysms of sexual climax. Prostitutes openly solicit passers-by. Hard drugs are a sideline sold by streetcorner hot dog vendors. Pornographic films, books, and pictures are openly on display.

Seemingly, nobody on Bourbon Street has heard of the Ten Commandments and the Sermon on the Mount.

In the midst of this desert of degradation, only one oasis exists. Crammed between a liquor store and a honky-tonk is the headquarters of the Chaplain of Bourbon Street. Walk through the wrought-iron gates and you are in another world. With contributions from all over the world, Harrington has painstakingly built a modern evangelistic mission crowded into a suite of four rooms.

Harrington, ordained to preach the gospel at the First Baptist Church of New Orleans, chose not to find himself a comfortable pastorate with a respectable and solvent congregation. He took the advice of one of his seminary

professors to seek out a "pocket of sin" and serve the Lord there.

"I couldn't find a bigger pocket of sin than Bourbon Street," he told me. So he opened up in the French Quarter before he had finished his seminary studies. Through persistence and dedication he gradually won the respect of the French Quarter power structure, primarily the nightclub owners. He also won the admiration of the hard-bitten, soul-sick residents who live and work in the Quarter.

Harrington has organized a capable staff, including Steve Callahan and Sally Stallings, which frees him to travel 100,000 miles a year to evangelize and bring people to Christ. He has been to Vietnam and Paris to preach his message of salvation. Wherever he goes, he wins hundreds, sometimes thousands, for the Lord.

But when Harrington is in New Orleans he preaches on Sundays at a "church" that resembles no other—the stage of the Sho-Bar nightclub across the street from his headquarters where strippers are the normal attraction. The club is run by the brother of Carlos Marcello, named by a national magazine as the head of the Louisiana Mafia.

Over 3,800 people crowded into the Hollywood Paladium in July, 1967.

I met many in New Orleans who had been converted by Harrington—alcoholics freed from the bottle, addicts rescued from narcotics, prostitutes now earning an honest living. I got the state, the feel, the smell and the atmosphere of Bourbon Street. And when I returned home my fingers flew over the typewriter, and soon our book, "The Chaplain of Bourbon Street," was finished. I wrote in white heat, inspired.

I often wonder what would have happened to me had I not met this evangelist who began life in Sweet Water, Alabama, rose to become a highly-paid insurance agent, then saw his marriage almost end in divorce before his conversion and dedication to the service of God.

There is no one in America like him. A reporter has called Harrington the "most unusual preacher of the twentieth century." He is a giant in evangelism who is becoming one of the most influential voices in America.

Because he introduced me to Jesus, tranquilizers are now a memory for me, I have since stopped seeing my psychiatrist and my feelings of anger and violence have disappeared. In my family, Bible reading, prayer and devotion to the principles of Christ are practiced every day.

And last July, after he and his charming wife, Joyce, came to Los Angeles to read the manuscript of the book, Harrington sent me my proudest possession, a red Bible.

"To my friend in Christ," Bob wrote on the dedication page. "I thank my Lord for allowing us to meet and to work together for his cause!"

To which I can only add: "Amen."

19. Build Yourself an Image

What makes people think of you?
What reminds people of you?
Do you have an image?

The answer to this last question is yes! All of us have some type of image. Maybe the public is not too conscious of it, but we have one. Right? What's yours?

Bob Harrington—Chaplain of Bourbon Street. This name and title have truly become one and the same.

As I write this chapter I'm in Houston, Texas with my family, Joyce, Rhonda and Mitzi, on one of our rare weekends together. Last night we enjoyed Houston's Rodeo with Elvis Presley as their guest artist. Now there's a man who has built such an image that when you think of rock and roll, or blue suede shoes, you think of Elvis (no last name needed). How did he do this so fast and then maintain his image? I'm seated next to a picture window on the ninth floor of the Warwick Hotel as I prayerfully share with you the importance of building a good, but yet dynamic image of yourself and your ministry to use for our Lord's glory.

By the way, don't let the devil get you hung up on this false humility bit of staying in the background. Expose who you are and what you are doing in every conceivable way. Don't let little thinking people keep you and your possible image under the bushel. Turn loose, man, and go-go for God.

As my good friend, President of the Southern Baptist Convention, Dr. W. A. Criswell, pastor of First Baptist Church, Dallas, said in one of his great books, "Look Up, Brother."

This Warwick Hotel in Houston has a world-wide image. It didn't come overnight, but it came. The City of Houston has quite a "fast-growing city" image. The citizens of this city are excited over what Houston has done, is doing and plans to do. Are people excited over your image?

I have been invited here by Dr. W. LeRay Fowler, Pastor of West University Baptist Church, to lead his people in a Sunday through Wednesday Crusade. It's my prayer that our ministry can do such a good job for Christ and His Church that this will help to lay more ground work toward a GREATER HOUSTON CRUSADE in the future. Saturday and Sunday I am to help Dr. Presnell Wood and his church, Park Place Baptist here in Houston. Let me share just one local instance as to how my image helps the local pastor. Looking on the religious page of the Houston *Post* I see a headline on Page 21 with this caption: "Noted Chaplain to Speak Here." This headline is over four columns of "Church News in Brief" including announcements of sixteen local churches. Why did they use my title in the headline? Because of the image! This title, "Chaplain of Bourbon Street" has become the sizzle to help me sell my steak. Looking over the advertisements of the many local churches I see in bold black print:

THE CHAPLAIN
OF BOURBON STREET
is coming to
PARK PLACE BAPTIST

No date, time, nor address is given. This teaser type of ad would not have been as effective without the image.

As I further scan this religious page, I see the name of a

God's Super Salesman

Baptist preacher who has built himself a real image. The key to his image has not been a title like mine or a gimmick like some but by persistent working at his calling. His name: John R. Bisagno, pastor of First Baptist Church, Houston, Texas. This young, dedicated preacher of the Gospel, first a musician, then surrendered to preach, in five years built an image for himself and God's glory, as pastor of Dell City, Oklahoma's First Southern Baptist Church, that no other Southern Baptist pastor could touch. He and his church led the convention in baptisms for the last three years. No wonder the people of First Church, Houston, wanted this man and his image for their church and city.

May I quickly add: you don't sit around and try to figure out a good image for yourself. The image develops as a by-product to your calling as you carry out the will of God in your life. When I first opened up on Bourbon Street in the French Quarter of New Orleans, Louisiana I had no idea or thought of this "Chaplain of Bourbon Street." The first time I put on a blood red tie I had no idea that the red tie, red socks,

Books help witness for Christ.

and red handkerchief would become my trademark. As we are faithful to God in our calling, these things seem to help shape our image.

Dr. Manuel Scott, black pastor of Calvary Baptist in Los Angeles, has an image. Sure he can preach. Yes, he has a sharp mind. But his crowd is always waiting to see him take both hands and rub his head, pull on and out his suspenders, and paw like a horse with his foot behind the pulpit. Maybe this looks crazy in print, or sounds crazy as you think about it, but it works.

More, if you don't mind (and you must not or you wouldn't have bought this book) about my image: this is what the editors of Doubleday Book Co. had to say concerning "The Chaplain of Bourbon Street." (Reprinted by *permission*).

He's been called the most unusual preacher of the twentieth century. And with good reason. His church is a stripper's emporium. His parishioners include dope addicts, prostitutes, alcoholics, homosexuals, and gangsters. His name is Reverend Bob Harrington, and his parish is New Orleans' Bourbon Street—the place Billy Graham has called "the middle of hell."

This is Bob Harrington's story, the autobiography of an extraordinary man told with great gusto and drama. We see him as an Alabama country boy, college student, Navy recruit, successful and cynical insurance salesman, and—after his dramatic conversion—as "a man on fire for God."

Build Yourself an Image —❦{129}❦—

Reverend Harrington, an ordained Baptist minister, drew some sharp criticism when, in 1961, he opened his mission on the most sin-soaked street in America, but he explains, "It's where the action is. Too many preachers sit in air-conditioned comfort in sanctum sanctorums and wait for people to come to them . . . these preachers should put more shoe leather in their salvation, they need more holy boldness." As one who truly practices what he preaches, Reverend Harrington, one of the most sought-after evangelists in America, travels over 100,000 miles a year delivering his soul-saving messages.

Flamboyant, controversial, and outspoken, the Chaplain of Bourbon Street stands out on the pages of this inspiring book—as do the many fascinating and colorful characters who are part of his everyday life. Reverend Harrington has said, "Every day of my life brings new adventure." And he's put it all down here—the adventures, the excitement, and, above all, the deep religious conviction that has made him a dedicated crusader for Christ.

. . . .

The word spread fast along Bourbon Street. No one had invited me—a sin-busting, devil-chasing young preacher—into the hellhole that was the French Quarter of New Orleans.

In the courtyard leading to my office, I hung a flaming red cross, bathed in a yellow spotlight, that could be seen clearly from the street. On the sidewalk I placed a wooden signboard that invited the lost, the damned, and the troubled inside for counseling, aid, prayer, and comfort.

The cross and the sign were an affront to the powerful, money-hungry owners of the honky-tonk strip joints and bars that front Bourbon Street like so many open manhole covers.

I was an interloper, a stranger who had no place in an area dedicated to perverted pleasure. Preaching the Lord's word in this heartland of heathenism was no way to win friends and influence people.

U. S. Coast Guard Chief Petty Officers' Luncheon, New Orleans, Louisiana hears the "Chaplain of Bourbon Street."

I knew that my ministry on Bourbon Street was going to be difficult. I had no illusions. But Mark's injunction, ". . . Go ye into all the world, and preach the gospel to every creature" strengthened my resolve.

Dr. John Rawlings, pastor of Landmark Baptist Temple, Cincinnati, Ohio, said, "It's easy to promote a revival when you have Bob Harrington as your evangelist. He has built such an image for himself that radio people want to talk to him, television people want to see him, and newspapers want to write about him." And I want to say that Brother John took full advantage of this image on my first visit to his church, getting me into schools, civic clubs, radio interviews, television appearances on "Bob Braun 50–50 Club," the Dennis Wholley Show, and the Phil Donahue Show. We hit over five night

clubs, and on and on. I have made return visits to his great soul-winning church many times since that first visit and we always have open doors to all the above mentioned outlets. AND IT'S ALL FREE (just years of work building an image that people can relate to)!

Here are some headlines from different cities and their newspapers. Did my image help in this coverage and witness?

Columbus, Georgia:
BOURBON STREET CHAPLAIN PREACHES AT NIGHT CLUB

Honolulu, Hawaii (*Honolulu Advertiser*):
HOW CHAPLAIN'S ACT FOLLOWS A STRIPPER

Dayton, Ohio (*Dayton Daily News*):
BROTHER BOB'S ON GO-GO FOR GOD

Alexandria, Louisiana (*Alexandria Daily Town Talk*):
**CHAPLAIN OF BOURBON STREET PRAISES U.S.
ROLE IN ASIA**

Atlanta, Georgia (front page of *The Atlanta Journal*)
**CHAPLAIN OF BOURBON STREET PREACHES
AMID GO-GO GIRLS**

San Antonio, Texas (*San Antonio Express/News*):
**GREEN GATE STRIPPERS HALT FOR LOOK AT
PEARLY GATES**

New Orleans, Louisiana (*Times-Picayune & States Item*):
**WHAT A FRIEND I HAVE IN JESUS,
SINGS STRIPPER**

Fort Worth, Texas (*Fort Worth Star-Telegram*):
MINISTER PROCLAIMS GOSPEL IN THE CELLAR

Lawton, Oklahoma (*The Lawton Constitution*):
FIERY PREACHER GOES "WHERE THE ACTION IS"

Detroit, Michigan (front page *The Detroit News*):
EVANGELIST REBUFFED IN BAR-STAGE TOUR
REVEREND BOB HUNTS LOST SOULS IN DETROIT
BOURBON STREET CHAPLAIN FAILS TO SAVE
SOULS IN DETROIT BARS
STRIPPERS SHUN EVANGELIST AS HE VISITS IN
DETROIT

Austin, Texas (*Austin American-Statesman*):
OFFBEAT CLERIC TO PREACH HERE

Las Vegas, Nevada (front page of *Review-Journal*):
COMPARED TO VEGAS—SODOM, GOMORRAH
"BUSH LEAGUE"

Associated Press (world-wide release):
PASTOR BEARDS SIN IN BOURBON DENS

United Press International:
BROTHER BOB PREACHES FROM STRIPPERS
STAGE

Chattanooga, Tennessee (*Free-Press*)
STANDING ROOM ONLY HEAR HARRINGTON IN
CITY AUDITORIUM

Build yourself a real solid image that can help to undergird
your calling (from God). Use it to the fullest to help bring
"God's kingdom on earth as it is in heaven."

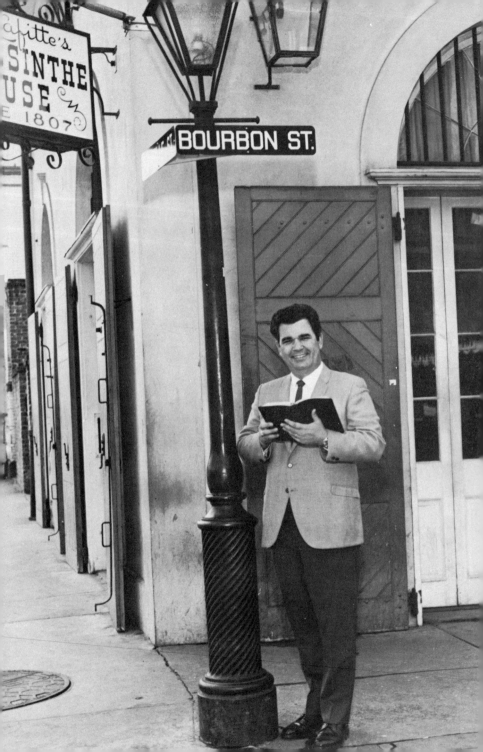

20. What Motivates Me?

Money is a great motivator to many. I must admit it plays an important part in my motivation. It's good to have a ministry that does not have a "we must have your money or close" image. It's good to have a home for my family at the age of forty-two paid for and mortgage free. It's good to have enough royalties from my first book "Chaplain of Bourbon Street," published by Doubleday, to pay for my older daughter, Rhonda Joyce's, four years in Baylor University. This, my second book, will pay for my other daughter, Mitzi Jayne's, college wherever she goes. But I had tremendous motivation before the house and book became a reality. I personally believe my true motivation comes from my love for Jesus and His desire to use me and keep me filled with the Holy Spirit of God.

I read in one of my sales manuals seven factors that motivate people:

1. The profit motive
2. The prestige motive
3. The pleasure motive
4. The imitation motive
5. The security motive
6. The convenience motive
7. The desire-to-avoid fear motive

Maybe many of these apply to you as they do to me. Look at the pleasure motive.

As a God-called evangelist, one who travels and preaches the gospel, many hours are spent alone. Sometimes in a lonely motel room, with my family in New Orleans, I say, "Bob, you must be crazy to leave your family and devote more than two-thirds of your life to others! Why?" Then here comes my motivation:

(Billy Grammar, country-music artist, in Nashville, during my September 1969 crusade, surrendered his life to Jesus and now is testifying all over America. James Welch, outstanding TV personality, now a lay-speaker for Christ. Letters from teen-age boys and girls thanking me for leading their dads to Christ, many saying that "he no longer drinks and cusses mother"). Sitting in on the ordination of young men into the ministry who were saved under our ministry. "Brother Bob, I came to your crusade and got saved." On and on my motivation continues. Praise the Lord for holy-led motivation.

Prestige plays a part in anyone's motivations. To be loved, respected, and thought well of is important. To live in the Lake Vista section of New Orleans out in the Lakeshore area with Mayor Schiro, Al Hirt, Pete Fountain, and others. (Across the street lives the chairman of the board of the National Bank of Commerce.) But with all of this, what the world calls prestige would be nothing but vanity (as Solomon said) if I didn't have holy motivation from my Lord and Saviour, Jesus Christ.

What motivates you?

What makes you read this book?

Mitzi, my younger daughter, motivates me as I see her developing into a dedicated young Christian lady. I am motivated when my friends tell me that she has been a blessing to their life. Billy Hill, who works in public relations with our ministry, is proud of a letter of encouragement Mitzi wrote him when she was just fifteen years of age but already a Queen-Regent in the

All ages hear Harrington.

Girls' Auxiliary of First Baptist Church.

Rhonda, my older daugher, motivates me as I see her live for Christ. On the night she became Queen-Regent in Service with the GA's of our church she stood gracefully behind the pulpit and said to the congregation, "I wonder where I would be tonight as a sixteen-year-old girl if Jesus had not saved my daddy's soul back in 1958." You talk about chill bumps or glory streaks going up and down your spine, I had them that night! If someone had snapped my shoe strings, I would have gone on to glory. This is *true Holy Ghost motivation!*

Joyce, my wife since January 18, 1947, motivates me as I see her getting such a thrill in life as a wife and mother. Three days after I was saved I began preaching, and Joyce had to start teaching school to supplement my income as my formative years in the ministry began. She taught until this year (1969–1970). Now she is a full-time wife and mother. It motivates me to see her dedication to Christ and his church. How she helps our daughters to discipline their time and talents for the glory of our Lord! How she leads the girls with their morning devotionals at the breakfast table!

I could go on and on with discussion of my family and the tremendous part they play in my personal motivation.

My pastor, *Dr. J. D. Grey,* First Baptist Church of New Orleans is a great motivator to my motivation. He is always an encouragement to me and my ideas—even when some seem a little way-out. He wrote Don McNeil in Chicago to have me on his breakfast club. He sent a letter to "Art Linkletter's House Party." He helped me with the liaison of going to Viet Nam. In one of his short notes to me, he said, "Bob, when you get ready to go to the moon, let me know who to write." Dr. Grey said of my being called an evangelist: "Here is a man truly on fire for God." Dr. Grey hired me as his assistant when I was just fourteen months old in the Lord. Later he recommended to our church that they ordain me into the ministry as

At the pulpit . . .

an "evangelist." While serving as assistant to Dr. Grey, I preached an eight-day revival in our church. Practically every time I get to go to our church with my family, which is too rare, my pastor calls on me to pray. Needless to say, "I love my pastor."

My mother and daddy (Rev. and Mrs. Robert C. Harrington, Methodist Church, Brent, Alabama), are real motivators to my motivation. They tried to offer my brother Jerry and me everything they could as we were growing up. I had the real joy of leading both of my parents (who have always been most religious but lost) to a saving knowledge in Christ. My dad was in his middle fifties at the time of his real conversion and at the age of 58 surrendered to preach the gospel as a minister in the Methodist Church. What a thrill this past Christmas when I was to preach in his church to see my mother at the organ, my daughter Rhonda at the piano, and my daddy at the pulpit to introduce me! Here is some of what he said: "Ladies and gentlemen, our speaker tonight is my son physically, but my father spiritually." Motivation? Is this some of it? Yes, praise the Lord.

In this chapter, "What Motivates Me?" I'm attempting to put it on paper—the things that keep me going. I am not attempting to tell you what motivates other people, but "what motivates me."

Rhonda and Mitzi Harrington are both "Queen Regents in Service" with GA's of First Baptist Church, New Orleans, Louisiana.

My dedicated staff help to motivate me to work harder for my Lord. May I introduce my staff, all soul-winners, to you:

Steve Callahan, Executive Director, who is a saved Baptist deacon, member of Beverly Hills Baptist Church of Dallas, Texas. Steve has a Masters degree in sales management from Harvard University. Steve and three others keep the home fires burning and a daily witness for Jesus on Bourbon Street in New Orleans. The other three are:

Mrs. Portia Bonham, Secretary and Soul-winner,
Rev. Ron Carter, Minister on the Street,
Pat Butler, Associate and soul-winner.

In addition to these four at home, there are three of us who travel most of the time in evangelistic services. I do the job of the evangelist, and *Jack Price,* formerly with Rev. Dickson Rial of Orchard Hills Baptist Church, Garland, Texas is my Music Coordinator. Jack is great in developing a crusade choir—fast, but effective. But he is even better in his solo work as he sings with his heart and soul in each song.

Then there's the one and only *Billy Hill,* my Alabama (Florence) Public Relations Director. Billy joined us after our successful Huntsville, Alabama crusade. He played college football at Mississippi State in Starkville. Then he helped Bear Bryant some at Bama. Billy is great in relating our ministry to the Fellowship of Christian Athletes, Campus Crusades, Youth for Christ, colleges, and high schools.

Success is a great motivator. Looking over last year's (1969) schedule is a motivation to me to do better in 1970. My 1969 year included:

    40 revivals in churches, auditoriums or stadiums
    97 civic clubs after-dinner messages
 2,670 radio messages (50 radio stations weekly)
    12 conventions
     7 autograph parties
    32 high schools

13 night clubs
5 colleges and universities
41 television appearances (many national)
3 appearances on Cathedral of Tomorrow (54 million viewers)

The dedication and determination of my Board of Directors to help me do *more* for our Christ is another motivation. May I introduce you, my friend, to this board.

1970 BOARD OF DIRECTORS
THE MINISTRY OF BOB HARRINGTON, INC.

Bob Harrington	W. D. Brunson
Joyce Harrington	Dan Hunter
Steve Callahan	Dr. Homer Watts
Bill Taylor	Stuart McClendon

My prayers are extended upward for authors! The hardest thing for me to do is sit down and write, but in writing this chapter on motivation I feel impressed to reflect back over the past twelve years and call a few names of people who have been used as motivators to me:

A. L. Weimorts, Eight Mile, Alabama: In my first months of building my ministry for Christ I would be down to my last dollar and in my mailbox would be a $50.00 or $100.00 check from this humble, dedicated man. As I write this book I recall that the watch on my left arm was a gift from Brother Al back in 1962. Thank you, Brother Weimorts.

Rev. Aubrey Mitchell, pastor of Highway 45 Baptist Church in Mobile, Alabama, invited me to preach a revival in his church while he was at Wilson Avenue Baptist in Prichard, Alabama. This was my first big church revival and my first big love offering ($500.00). While some of my fellow Southern Baptist pastors in the Mobile area chose either to ignore me or to discourage me, Brother Aubrey had his church to back me and support my little tent revivals around Mobile. This fundamental independent church helped to open doors all through the U.S.A. Thanks, Brother Aubrey.

Dr. J. D. Allen, pastor of First Baptist Church, Plateau, Alabama, invited me to be the evangelist for his church during the 1958 simultaneous revivals. This was my first revival in a Southern Baptist Convention church. Over one hundred were saved, and we had to extend the meeting for more than the scheduled week. Dr. Allen is on the staff of the Baptist Bible Institute in Graceville, Florida, at this time. Thanks, Dr. Allen.

Ed Folsom, at the time of my conversion was pastoring Central Baptist in Dixon Mills, Alabama (six miles east of Sweet Water). Ed put me on radio testifying, took me to jails and prisons, drove me to Bob Jones University to a Bible Conference. There I heard Dr. Jack Hyles. Brother Ed had me preach a revival in his church one month after I was saved. Thanks, Ed.

B. B. Blackwell, local business man in Chickasaw, Alabama, who had just lost his only son, moved into help me as crusade manager. We bought a furniture delivery truck and painted it up as our crusade "Gospel Wagon." Braxton helped to set up and direct our "Coffeeville Crusade" and our "Pensacola Crusade" where for five weeks we preached under the big tent. Cy Ramseyer led the singing during this great crusade. Thanks, Braxton.

Four men of Mobile and Chickasaw who wanted to encourage and help my ministry went on my note at the First Commercial Bank of Chickasaw and later they paid off this note for me. The men are: *W. D. Brunson, V. N. Evans, Lawrence C. Miller,* and *Dr. W. A. Ritchie.* Thanks, men.

Two men in the Mobile Christian Business Men's Committee who were always a motivation to me are: *T. Massey Bedsole,* attorney, and *Tom Martin,* executive with G. M. and O.

Railroads. They both helped me to develop the first "Thank you, Lord" day in Mobile with services in the town square. Mr. Martin, son of the great evangelist of yesteryears, T. T. Martin, was the man who notified Dr. J. D. Grey of New Orleans that I was coming to seminary. Thanks, men.

My first few months in New Orleans would have been more of a strain had it not been for *Robert and Peggy Barnett.* Robert bought my tape recorder and Peggy helped in my office on Bourbon Street without pay when it was hard to pay the rent. One night Robert drove me to Starkville, Mississippi for a meeting because I had no other way of going. Thanks, friends.

At one time on Bourbon Street I was two months behind with my rent and radio broadcast payments and God sent a lady I'd never met before by my office with a $1,000.00 check. Thanks, *Mrs. R. N. Myers.*

I needed a car; all we had was a little Ford Falcon and it needed prayer. At the close of my Ponchatoula crusade, two friends went to the bank in Hammond, Louisiana and borrowed the money to buy me a new Ford XL and many others

in the area helped to make the payments on it. Thanks, *Bernard Lavigne and Blanche McLin.*

Is this motivation? Praise the Lord!

Floyd Cook, while he was living in Sweet Water, Alabama, across the street from the church where I was saved, had me come back one night to my hometown for a testimonial dinner in my honor and to preach the next day in the church where I met Jesus. Thanks, Floyd.

I don't want you to think that I'm getting carried away with human motivators in my personal motivation because my main source of motivation comes from the grace of God my Father, Jesus Christ my Saviour, and the precious Holy Spirit, my Comforter and Teacher. But it still takes the human instruments to keep you going for HIM. If I had to narrow down my list of names to one person my Lord used to help motivate me *most,* that one man would have to be my dear friend, *Fred Roan,* a saved automobile dealer in Mobile, Alabama. Fred taught me how to pray and witness for my new Saviour. It was through Fred I was invited to preach a week's revival

at the Mobile Rescue Mission, where *Clyde Reynolds* is Director. *Luke McDaniels* led the singing in that meeting and many more during my first year with Christ. It was Fred who took me to Laurel, Mississippi to hear Evangelist, *Eddie Martin*, who later asked to do advance work with his team in city-wide crusades. Fred used to have me appear on his television program in Mobile. He would take me around to testify with him to church groups and others. Later, after I had entered the New Orleans Baptist Seminary and had begun my work as Chaplain of Bourbon Street, Fred introduced me to *W. A. Taylor, Sr.*, Taylor Machine Works in Louisville, Mississippi, who in turn introduced me to his son *Bill Taylor*, who serves as a member of our Board of Directors and Vice President of our nonprofit corporation. Then Bill Taylor introduced me to *Rev. Jimmy Stroud*, Director of Memphis Union Mission in Memphis, Tennessee who had me for a revival and suggested my first LP record and named it "Laughter, Truth and Music." On and on I could go concerning the vital part *Fred Roan*, a Baptist layman deacon has played in my motivation. Thanks, Fred.

I've read books on motivation, and I know many definitions of motivation, but I have attempted to show you motivation at its best in my life and ministry.

Do you remember some of the people who have helped to motivate you toward success?

I do. Like:

Captain Bob Sparks, U.S. Navy, who drops me a little note once in a while with a personal check enclosed.

Elbert Mullis, Dublin, Georgia, one of my forty-two radio sponsors, who had his Civitan Club to use me as their International Convention Speaker.

Charles Hogan, Newport News, Virginia who served as General Chairman of that great crusade and led his people to help finance my Washington, D.C. "Wake-Up America" rally in the Statler-Hilton Hotel Ballroom where the Lord led *Jack Allen,* barber from the House of Representatives, into our life. Jack opened the doors for me to become personal friends with Congressman Mendel Rivers of South Carolina and Melvin Laird, Secretary of Defense. Jack also was the instrument God used to get me to lead the House of Representatives in their opening prayer. Thanks, Charlie and Jack.

First Baptist Church, Milan, Tennessee, where Rev. Denzel Dukes is pastor, after a great eight-day church crusade, his people put another $2,000.00 in my ministry to help open up California, which it did. Art Linkletter Show and the Joe Pyne Show, plus a one-night rally in the Grand Ballroom of the Beverly Hilton Hotel in Beverly Hills. This led to a church meeting with *Dr. J. Thurmond George* in El Monte, California, then into two area wide crusades that climaxed in the Hollywood Palladium with over 3,000 in attendance. Now Dr. George is vice-president of California Baptist College, Riverside, California where he has invited me to speak to the students and to serve on their board of development. Thus the State of California is wide open to our ministry.

Many times I am asked the question concerning my ministry and its growth, "Bob, how did you do it?" Maybe after reading this chapter you'll find out it wasn't Bob but our Lord working through me and many of his people that has brought us to where we are. *"To God Be the Glory."*

21. He Keeps Me Preaching

Steve Callahan takes care of all non-preaching details for me. (This article was printed and released by *Christian Times,* July 27, 1969, written by Dwight M. Hooten. Reprinted by permission.)

Satan operates a highly successful business on New Orleans Bourbon Street, trafficking in concentrated sin and instant corruption.

Believing that Satan shouldn't have a corner on souls, Bob Harrington intruded upon his territory in 1961. Unsuccessful in devious ways to dislodge the fiery preacher, Satan's recent hope has been that success itself will be the means of failure . . . let a preacher get bogged down in details and he won't have time to be an effective preacher!

But that's not working with Bob Harrington, the Chaplain of Bourbon Street! It's now the job of a former devil's advocate to keep the chaplain preaching.

Steve Callahan, born in 1940 in Worcester, Massachusetts, stopped going to church at the age of 17. God just wasn't for him.

The business world had always fascinated Steve. Boston University's high standard in business education attracted him, but his father would not give his consent

Steve Callahan
"keeps Bob
preaching."

because BU was not a Catholic school. Steve went any-
way, and family support was cut off. Self support was no
problem. By his senior year he was earning well over
$12,000 annually. Except for essentials the money was
"blown" on weekends.

At age 20, Steve acted as John F. Kennedy's presi-
dential campaign manager for all of Worcester County,
Mass., taking on full responsibility for this county of three
quarters of a million people, and still lacking one year
from the voting age!

"Campaign manager, student, kicker. This kept me pushing well over 70 hours a week," Steve recalls. "The week-end flings became pretty well stereotyped—numbers racket, money, drink, women." He coveted more money, more power, and more influence that would make the satisfaction of any desire, and lust, a foregone conclusion.

But even at this stage, steeped in sin and depravity, Steve was unwittingly moving in an aura of influence destined to draw him closer and closer to divine will. God made a subtle move, causing astutely analytical Steve to make a miscalculation. He calculated that if the purpose and direction he was now looking for weren't coming from money, liquor, women, and gambling in Boston, he had better try another city.

Generally discriminating, and financially able to be fastidious, Steve looks back with thrill and wonderment that he took the first apartment he looked at in Dallas, Texas.

But, Boston hadn't been the problem. "What's wrong?" was become a recurring question. Life was running downhill, driverless, and without rein.

By the age of 24 Steve's eyes were clouded and his ears deaf to any of life's beauty of joy. Even life's ugliness was not much fun anymore. He was at a critical stage.

Steve needed a challenge. He always reacted well to challenges. He bet a friend $25 that Faye, a 22-year-old American Airlines hostess living in his apartment building, would yield as putty in his "experienced" hands. Faye had come from Knoxville, Tennessee, where her father pastored a Baptist Church. "She was different," Steve recalls. He added with apparent pride in Faye: "She wouldn't budge an inch!"

Steve's theory was to date a girl once, then move on to

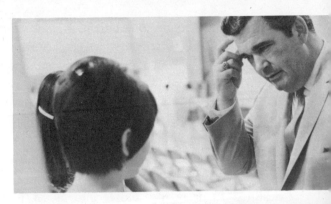

another. But they were all alike. Faye was different! Here was a kick of a far different sort—fun, refreshing.

Faye's pastor became concerned over this continued relationship and wrote to Faye's father.

What would Faye's father do? Wire for her to come home? Fly to Dallas, or phone the local pastor to call her in for some fast counselling? Satisfied that the Lord was round about his daughter as the mountains are round about Jerusalem, his kind admonition was: "It's safe to leave Faye alone," adding reassuringly, "she's okay."

Faye's Spirit-led witnessing soon began to break through. Witness! Steve now knows where he would be had it not been for a God-directed witness of a God-directed life.

He firmly believes that God caused Faye to come from Knoxville and caused him to come from Boston to converge upon that particular apartment house in Dallas. "Too many things fell in just right. Too unbelievable a change took place, to be coincidental," he firmly asserts. God had given Faye the gift for playing each move carefully. Steve wasn't asking to be saved. He didn't even know he was lost.

For the final move, God called several warriors into play. "I was conscious that Faye was executing a few adroit maneuvers, but," Steve smiles broadly as he recalls, "I didn't know all those people at church were praying for me!"

Still running from himself, weighted down with a

mounting undefined burden, Steve had reached a dead end of despondency! Alone in his apartment, he dropped to his knees and cried. He couldn't pray. He had no Bible. He phoned Faye's pastor. "I'll come right over." The pastor was ready to deal with these early signs of travail and birth. "No, don't come over. I just wanted to talk to you." The pastor prayed. Steve hung up.

Back on his knees and still weeping, the birth struggle continued agonizingly for hours. Not one cry, not one tear had gone unnoticed. Steve suddenly knew he was not alone: "Come unto me . . . and I will give you rest . . . my burden is light."

A new life began. A life yet without plans, but not without purpose and promised direction. Light had come into a dark and evil life, and Faye had borne witness of that Light. Witness. A new and vitally significant word for Steve.

"The next Sunday, I walked down the aisle of Faye's church and told them all that happened," Steve still recalls with enthusiasm. His urge for whiskey stopped immediately, but his beer habit lasted for several months. The body had grown used to soaking up large volumes of liquor. Faye recognized the problem, so when she left for work in the mornings, she mixed jugs of iced tea and filled his refrigerator with them. With this help, that victory was finally won.

It took even longer with the pipe and cigar, "But," Steve admits, "the tongue was the last to fall. These words were there and would flip right out."

Two years after joining the church, he and Faye were married by Faye's father. All of this resulted in a complete breach with his family. "I sense a gradual warming up," Steve says hopefully after two and a half years, "I only pray the Lord gives me enough time."

God's Super Salesman

Shortly after the wedding, Steve and Faye went on a safari to Africa. Africa made him somewhat missionary-minded. Should that be his field? He turned to Faye and said, "We'd better do some serious praying."

The answer unfolded fast. The Chaplain of Bourbon Street needed someone to relieve him of the mounting administrative responsibility which had skyrocketed since he first opened his office in the French Quarter of New Orleans. Was Steve interested? Naturally! He phoned his acceptance.

It's a big job with heavy responsibility. The nightly work on Bourbon Street alone takes three full-time evangelists. The chaplain's office phone number is on strippers' dressing room doors all through the area. Dancers, bartenders, club owners, and barkers make urgent use of it in frantic search for help.

Mothers, fathers, sons, daughters, running from the fringes of hell at home, gravitate to the very "center of hell" on Bourbon Street.

Alvin Roy, Strength Coach for the Kansas City Chiefs, checks out Bob's physical condition.

This work receives priority. Witness. Care is taken to see that it doesn't lag.

Steve's primary task is to keep the chaplain preaching, but he's dedicated to seeing that, as he puts it, "The lost get saved, and the saved live like it."

Steve Callahan has a definite idea of how the saved should live, not forgetting what it took to number him among them. He was at the barber shop when I called to interview him for this story, and showed up considerably beyond the appointed hour. I met him crossing Bourbon Street. "Hi," he waved with one of his frequent and easy smiles, "I went to get a hair-cut and got to witnessing to some people."

They travel with Bob.
(LEFT) Jack Price
(RIGHT) Billy Hill

He Keeps Me Preaching ---◦∘⊰{159}⊱∘◦---

Holiday Inn
OF AMERICA
MACON WELCOMES
BOB HARRINGTON
CHAPLAIN OF BOURON ST

22. Stay on Your "Holy Honeymoon"

Someone told me the reason I have not cooled down spiritually or compromised with the world is because I haven't left my first love. I don't want my "Holy Honeymoon" ever to end. Fred Roan, saved automobile dealer in Mobile, said, "I believe you can stay so close to Jesus while you are living and serving him that when the time comes for you to die you won't even feel the shift, it will be like a fluid drive going on into heaven."

Since my new-birth date in 1958 I don't remember one day I failed to mention getting saved, plus when and were it happened. In all my messages to crusades, civic clubs, churches, schools, nightclubs, etc., I always refer to "when it happened."

Each time I sign my name, Bob Harrington, I put by it or under it, saved 4-15-58.

In one of my last insurance policy applications I had the agent include my second birth-date.

On my tombstone one day will be:

Bob Harrington
A Saved-God Called Preacher of the Gospel
Born	**September 2, 1927**
Born Again	**April 15, 1958**
Died	**He Didn't**
Transferred	**(date)**

In my house we celebrate both of my birthdays. Don't leave your first love.

The most unhappy people I meet in my travels are not the lost hell-bound sinners. This type of person doesn't really know what unhappiness is because he has never been truly happy. The most unhappy person I meet is the saved person who has left or even ignored his first-love.

Stay on your Holy-Honeymoon! Remember: You and I, the saved, are the bride of Christ and thank God he is the Bridegroom.

Many times in my preaching I make this statement: "I'd rather die today rightly in love with Christ than to be a has-been, used-to-be, or a drop-out tomorrow." May I go a little further in this thought? "I'd rather die than to become a liberal in the work of my Lord." I'm sure this statement will provoke laughter on some of our liberals today, but they need to laugh once in awhile. I'm sure this type of statement will bring many Amen's from men and women who have not left their "Holy-Honeymoon."

Dr. Vance Havner, outstanding Bible preacher from Greenville, South Carolina, stirs my soul with his message "Don't Lose the Wonder." He makes reference to people getting saved and excited about it, and then they soon get over it. I've been saved and excited for twelve years, and it's my prayer that I never get over it.

Many of my Christian friends can shout "Praise the Lord" and "Amen" while things are going good, but, let some bad come, and they doubt their salvation. When I accepted Christ as my Saviour (bridegroom) I became his bride. This is very similar to my getting married to Joyce. I committed myself to her and she to me for better or for worse, sickness or health, until death. My Lord is my Saviour through good and bad, mountain tops and valleys, health and sickness, happy times and sad. My salvation is not based on my personal feelings, but my personal faith in Jesus Christ. May I quickly add—it surely does feel good to be saved,

K.L.U. (keep looking up) is a great saying of Dr. E. T. Norman, a saved medical doctor in Greensboro, Alabama. Saved late in life, this outstanding witness for Christ does many things to keep on his "Holy Honeymoon," such as: hand out tracts, pick up and witness to hitchhikers, preach everywhere, write to the mailman on the envelopes of his letter, and nail up signs along the highways. I believe one of these signs on the highway between my hometown of Sweet Water, Alabama and Linden, Alabama had a tremendous effect on my life before my conversion. This sign was *"HAPPY IS THE MAN WHO KNOWS GOD."* I knew as I saw and read this sign many times, as a married college student, that I was not a happy man. Thank you, Dr. Norman, for the important part you have played in my life and ministry.

In my daily life as a saved man, husband, daddy, and God-called preacher, I try to practice the continual presence of Christ. He is with me always and will *never, never* forsake me. Many times I include him in my conversation as if he and I were having dialogue. Sometimes in the morning, as I wake up to begin a new day, I greet my Lord with "Good morning, Jesus, I love you and want to thank you for another good night's rest." I try to let the last thing I think or say at night as I go to sleep be, "Good night Jesus, thanks for taking care of my family and me during this day. I'll see you in the morning."

Sometimes, when I feel the response will be good, when I'm asked, "Bob, how do you feel?" I answer, "Saved and happy in the Lord."

As I write part of this chapter, I'm in flight to Dayton, Ohio for my second confrontation with Madalyn Murray O'Hair, the atheist from Austin, Texas, considered the most hated woman in America. This is the second time this week for us to appear on the Phil Donahue Show originating from WLWD, Dayton,

Ohio. I had no weapon to use on my first show except my love for Jesus and his love for me. You can't knock this type of sincere witness for Christ. I don't want to argue about my faith in him or her lack of faith. I just stick to my personal testimony and the blood of the Lamb. I remember my second visit on the Joe Pyne Show in Hollywood. We were about ten minutes into the interview and Joe said, "Slow down man, you're the first man ever on my program I've had to hold back." I answered, "I'm probably the first man you've had on your show who knew where he was going." It's that dynamic first love ("Holy Honeymoon") we who are saved have that the lost cannot understand or even compete with. Keep your first love for Jesus so active it will become contagious. Stephen, the first martyr, died with his face displaying that his "Holy Honeymoon" was not ending even with death. The apostle Paul, who never left his first love even though he feared becoming a castaway, had so real a first love for Christ when he witnessed to the world leaders in his day that they would say "thou almost persuaded me to become a Christian."

Billy Graham has never left his "Holy Honeymoon." His audience can feel it in his voice and see it in his eyes.

Oral Roberts has never forgotten what Jesus did for him as a young man. As I visited with Mr. Roberts on the campus of

Oral Roberts University in Tulsa, Oklahoma the first love for
Jesus could be felt through his countenance and even the atmosphere of the campus made me feel at home.

Many God-called preachers today are going into secular
work, bond selling programs, public relations, school teaching, and so forth, because they got over their Holy-Honeymoon. Preachers, don't let the devil talk you outside of the hill
of God for your life. He sometimes will use your closest friends
or even your wife to lure you, as Samson was, away from loving Jesus.

Keep a daily love in your heart and life for Jesus!

Here is my formula for keeping on my "Holy-Honeymoon"
(Bob's Five Point Plan):

> First—I read at least one chapter in my Bible each
> day.
>
> Second—I pray at least ten minutes each day.
>
> Third—I talk to someone each day about Jesus.
>
> Fourth—I leave a Bible open in my home and office.
>
> Fifth—We pray together in my family.

Active church life will be the results of this formula carried
out in your life. Faithfulness as a tither will result. I tithe

through my Sunday School into the ministry of First Baptist Church, New Orleans. Each member of my born-again staff is a tither, not to my ministry, but in his church.

Here's a good outline to preach (given to me by Rev. Mike Dawson of Charleston, South Carolina). I preached it this morning at Northwest Baptist Church, Miami, Florida, where Bill Chapman is pastor.

(Home Board Photo)

THREE THINGS THAT MAKE A DIFFERENCE

First—The Christ you Meet
Second—The Conviction you Seek
Third—The Company you Keep
Preach it!
Practice it!

23. If I Were You!

In this book I have tried to put me, my life, and my ministry on paper. It has been most difficult—to say the least. But if one of my thoughts, ideas, metaphors, or simple suggestions has been of some help to you and your life for Christ, then the hours spent in writing this, my second book, have been well used for His glory.

Anne Heywood said: "We must treat ideas somewhat as though they were baby fish. Throw thousands out into the waters. Only a handful will survive, but that is plenty." Needless to say; but, I have tried hundreds of ideas and some of those I have considered fruitful I've shared with you.

Josiah Royce said: "Thinking is like loving and dying. Each of us must do it for himself."

Would you like to be a "real" success in life? You can be, if you will determine in your heart to be!

The greatest opportunities that the world has ever known lies before you today. There is more work to do now than there ever has been in the history of the world!

The population of the world today is greater than it ever has been; there is estimated to be over a thousand million souls (one billion) who have never heard the name of Jesus Christ, and millions and millions of others who have heard, but who have not been "born again" as Jesus said was necessary before anyone could enter into the kingdom of heaven. When you realize that without believing in Christ, as the Scripture has said, that no man can be saved; that no man has any true hopes of ever reaching Heaven, but is destined to spend eternity with the lost and damned; how it ought to stir our innermost emotions, and cause us to determine in our hearts to try to get the gospel to "every creature," as Jesus commanded us to do, as quickly as possible.

With all of our modern means of printing, radio, and television that we have today, if the Christian people would only stir themselves, we could soon get the gospel to these many souls. Will you dedicate yourself to work for the "King of Kings and Lord of Lords," the Lord Jesus Christ? Will you determine to be a "real" success in your life?

Please receive this message of warning from a friend who wants you to be saved from the wrath and judgments of God, that are soon coming upon all sinners and unbelievers; upon all who refuse to believe upon his Son Jesus Christ and be saved. The most important thing in your life is to prepare to meet God. "What shall a man give in exchange for his soul?" (Matt. 16:26).

God is a God of love, He is not willing that any should perish, but that all should have everlasting life. However, He is also a God of Justice; all sin and disobedience must therefore be punished and God has decreed that it shall be punished with an ETERNAL PUNISHMENT, unless an atonement is made for it. There can be no atonement, or forgiveness of sins, except through the shedding of blood by someone who is Holy and without sin. "Without shedding of blood [there] is no remission" (Heb. 9:22). The only way that God, in his justice, could forgive our sins, was for someone else, without sin, to die in our place. In his great love and mercy, God sent down from heaven his only begotten Son, Jesus Christ, who was born of a virgin, and was without sin, to die upon the Cross of Calvary, as an atonement for our sins, if we will only believe in Him, and accept Him as our Saviour.

There are certain conditions, however, that God requires us

to meet. He has done his part, now we must do ours. In the beginning of his ministry, Jesus told the people to "Repent: for the kingdom of heaven is at hand" (Matt. 4:17). It was necessary for the people to repent of their sins and to believe on him as their Saviour. All through his divine, miraculous life of ministry; preaching, teaching, healing the sick and afflicted, raising the dead, doing all the miracles and wonderful works which he did—finally dying upon the Cross for our sins —his purpose was "to seek and to save that which was lost" if they would only believe. Hear his sweet words of invitation, "Come unto me, all ye that labour and are heavy laden, and I will give you rest. Take my yoke upon you, and learn of me; for I am meek and lowly in heart: and ye shall find rest unto your souls. For my yoke is easy, and my burden is light" (11:28–30). Weary soul, you can find rest if you will only come to Him.

After his crucifixion upon the cross of Calvary, and his resurrection from the dead, Jesus told his disciples to "Go ye into all the world, and preach the gospel to every creature. He that believeth and is baptized shall be saved; but he that believeth not shall be damned" (Mark 16:15–16). Peter, that great apostle, in preaching to the people on the day of Pentecost after Jesus had ascended back into heaven after his resurrection, told the people to "Repent, and be baptized every one of you in the name of Jesus Christ for the remission of sins, and ye shall receive the gift of the Holy Ghost" (Acts 2:38). The apostle Paul preached "Believe on the Lord Jesus Christ and thou shalt be saved" (Acts 16:31). The prophet Isaiah said, "Let the wicked forsake his way, and the unrighteous man his thoughts: and let him return unto the Lord, and he will have mercy upon him; and to our God, for he will abundantly pardon" (55:7).

We see therefore, that in order to be saved, we must repent of our sins, and believe on this Lord Jesus Christ as our personal Saviour. Repentance implies that the Holy Spirit has convicted us of our sins, of righteousness, and of the judgment to come, and that we are sorry from the bottom of our hearts, that we have sinned against God; we are willing to confess and forsake all of our sins, and to make any restitution that God may require, in order to put our souls right with Him. After you have done your part—after you have wholeheartedly repented of your sins—then you can look up to God in prayer,

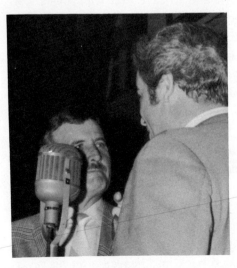

Archie Campbell and the Grand Ole Opry

(PAGE 173) Teenagers gather to pray for an injured friend

believing and accepting the Lord Jesus Christ as your personal Saviour, and believe from your heart that God forgives you of all your sins, according to his promises. Jesus said, "Him that cometh to me I will in no wise cast out."

Wouldn't you like to become a child of God, knowing that your sins are all forgiven, and that you are ready to die, or for Jesus to come? You can, if you will only believe and do what God requires you to do. "Though your sins be as scarlet, they shall be as white as snow; though they be red like crimson, they shall be as wool." (Isa. 1:18): Jesus is now at the right hand of God in heaven, and he will forgive you if you will come to him with your whole heart. You do not have to be in a church to be saved, although an old-fashioned church altar is an excellent place to find God. Go to your room, out in the woods, anywhere alone with God, pour out your heart and soul to him in great earnestness and sincerity; tell him how sorry you are that you have sinned, and mean it from the depth of your heart, and ask him to forgive you, and he will do it. You must be willing to confess and forsake all of your sins,

If I Were You —⋇(173)⋇—

and to make any restitution that is necessary. "If we confess our sins, he is faithful and just to forgive us our sins, and to cleanse us from all unrighteousness" (1 John 1:9). Pray until you KNOW that you are saved; until the Spirit of God bears witness with your spirit that you are a child of God.

Do not let anyone deceive you that you can be saved and go to heaven in any other way than the Bible teaches. There are many deceptions and false religions in the world today. Joining some church, trying to be good by your own good works, good morals, OR ANY OTHER BELIEF will not save us—IT TAKES THE BLOOD OF JESUS CHRIST—being "born again" through God's grace and forgiveness; Jesus said, "Ye must be born again" (John 3:7). The Bible says, "If any man be in Christ, he is a new creature: old things are passed away; behold all things are become new" (2 Cor. 5:17). Study the Bible—it alone is the WORD OF GOD. Jesus said, "Search the scriptures; for in them ye think ye have eternal life" (John 5:39). Read it carefully, prayerfully, reverently and consistently. Remember, it is God's Word to mankind, written under the inspiration of the Holy Spirit; "Holy men of God spake as they were moved by the Holy Ghost" (2 Peter 1:21). It is forever settled in heaven; not a single word will ever fail. All of its promises, warnings and teachings are absolutely true. Jesus said, "Heaven and earth shall pass away, but my words shall not pass away" (Matt. 24:35).

Your eternal destiny is at stake. Millions and millions of years (there is no end to eternity) you are to spend either in the lake of fire and brimstone with the sinners and unbelievers, suffering the torments of the damned, or in heaven, enjoying the bliss and happiness of the redeemed. If you are saved, if you have believed on the Lord Jesus Christ, accepted Him as your personal Saviour, and lived faithful and true to him, then heaven will be your eternal home, where there is no more sin, sorrow, sickness or death. "Eye hath not seen, nor ear heard, neither have entered into the heart of man, the things which God hath prepared for them that love him" (1 Cor. 2:9). (To get some idea of heaven please read the twenty-first chapter of Revelation, the last book in the Bible.) Now, precious soul, won't you please repent of your sins, give Jesus your heart, and live the rest of your life for him? How happy you will be through the countless ages of eternity for having done so!

After you are saved, then follow your Lord in water baptism, attend regularly some good, spiritual, fundamental church of your choice. Enjoy the worship of God and the fellowship of Christian people of like faith. Pray daily and study your Bible diligently, thereby growing in grace and in the knowledge of our Lord Jesus Christ. May God bless you and help you to be a faithful whole-hearted Christian, loving your Heavenly Father, and your Lord and Saviour Jesus Christ, with all of your heart, through time and eternity.

If I were you, I'd get saved and live like it for the glory of God!

Design for this book attempts to portray the nature of the ministry of "The Chaplain of Bourbon Street." The text is set in 11 point Times Roman for ease of readability; the widespread use of photographs is intended to facilitate ease of understanding the personal impact of this evangelist.

Format design: Dixon Waters

Dust-jacket design: Tom P. Seale
Jacket photograph: Robert Jackson

---•◦{176}◦•---   *God's Super Salesman*